MICHELIN

Chicago

must SEES

Chief Editor	Cynthia Clayton Ochterbeck
Senior Editor	M. Linda Lee
Writer	Meg Moss
Production Coordinator	Allison M. Simpson
Cartography	Peter Wrenn
Photo Editor	Brigitta L. House
Photo Research	Martha Hunt
Documentation	Doug Rogers
Typesetting	Octavo Design — Apopka, Florida
Cover Design	Paris Venise Design — Paris, 17e
Printing and Binding	Colonial Press International, Inc. — Miami, Florida

Contact us:
Michelin North America, One Parkway South, Greenville, SC 29615 USA
800-423-0485
www.michelintravel.com
email: Michelin.Guides@us.michelin.com

Manufacture française des pneumatiques Michelin
Société en commandite par actions au capital de 304 000 000 EUR
Place des Carmes-Déchaux – 63 Clermont-Ferrand (France)
R.C.S. Clermont-FD B 855 800 507

Note to the reader:
While every effort is made to ensure that all information in this guide is correct and up-to-date, Michelin Travel Publications (Michelin North America, Inc.) accepts no liability for any direct, indirect or consequential losses howsoever caused so far as such can be excluded by law.
Admission prices listed for sights in this guide are for a single adult, unless otherwise specified.

Special Sales:
For information regarding bulk sales, customized editions and premium sales, please contact our
Customer Service Departments: **USA** – 800-423-0485   **Canada** – 800-361-8236

Welcome to Chicago

Table of Contents

Table of Contents

THE MICHELIN STARS

For more than 75 years, travelers have used the Michelin stars to take the guesswork out of planning a trip. Our star-rating system helps you make the best decision on where to go, what to do, and what to see. A three-star rating means it's one of the "absolutelys"; two stars means it's one of the "should sees"; and one star says it's one of the "sees"—a must if you have the time.

★★★ Absolutely Must See
★★ Really Must See
★ Must See

Sights below are located in Chicago unless otherwise noted.

Three-Star Sights

Art Institute of Chicago★★★
Auditorium Building★★★
Carson Pirie Scott & Company★★★
Cloud Gate★★★
Field Museum of Natural History★★★
Jay Pritzker Pavilion★★★
John G. Shedd Aquarium★★★
John Hancock Center★★★
The Loop★★★
Magnificent Mile★★★
Millennium Park★★★
Museum Campus★★★
Museum of Science and Industry★★★
Oak Park★★★
Sears Tower★★★

Two-Star Sights

Adler Planetarium★★
Astor Street★★
Baha'i House of
   Worship★★ (Wilmette)
BP Bridge★★
Brookfield Zoo★★
Buckingham Fountain★★
Chicago Botanic
   Garden★★(Glencoe)
Chicago Cultural Center★★
Crown Fountain★★
860-880 North
   Lake Shore Drive★★
Federal Center★★
Frank Lloyd Wright Home
   and Studio★★ (Oak Park)
Graceland Cemetery★★
Grant Park★★
James R. Thompson Center★★
John Jacob Glessner House★★

Lincoln Park★★
Lincoln Park Zoo★★
Marquette Building★★
Monadnock Building★★
Navy Pier★★
Newberry Library★★
North Shore★★
Oriental Institute★★
Reliance Building★★
Richard J.
   Daley Center★★
River North★★
Robie House★★
Rookery★★
Tribune Tower★★
Unity Temple★★
   (Oak Park)
University of Chicago★★
Wrigley Building★★

One-Star Sights

Bailly Homestead and Chellberg Farm and Trail★ (Indiana Dunes National Lakeshore)
Charnley-Persky House★
Chicago Board of Trade Building★
Chicago Children's Museum★
Chicago Historical Society★
Chicago Water Tower and Pumping Station★
David and Alfred Smart Museum of Art★
The Drake Hotel★
Dune Succession Trail★ (Indiana Dunes National Lakeshore)
Forest Avenue★ (Oak Park)
Fourth Presbyterian Church★
Frank W. Thomas House★ (Oak Park)
Garfield Park Conservatory★
Gold Coast★
Henry B. Clarke House★
Illinois & Michigan Canal National Heritage Corridor★
Indiana Dunes National Lakeshore★
InterContinental Chicago★
Jane Addams Hull-House Museum★
Lincoln Park/DePaul★
Lockport★
Lurie Garden★
Marina City★
Marshall Field's★
Menomonee Street★
Michigan Avenue Bridge★
Morton Arboretum★ (Lisle)
Mount Baldy★ (Indiana Dunes National Lakeshore)
Museum of Contemporary Art★
Oak Street★
Old Town★
Ottawa★
Peggy Notebaert Nature Museum★
Pioneer Settlement★ (Lockport)
"Pleasant Home"★ (Oak Park)
Prairie Avenue Historic District★
Pullman Historic District★
Riverwalk★
Smith Museum of Stained-Glass Windows★
State Street★
Streeterville★
Water Tower and Pumping Station★
Water Tower Place★
West Beach Area★ (Indiana Dunes National Lakeshore)
Wrigley Field★

Listed below is a selection of Chicagoland's most popular annual events. Please note that dates may change from year to year. For more detailed information, contact the Chicago Office of Tourism: 312-744-2400 or www.cityofchicago.org.

January

Winter Delights   312-744-3370
Various locations (Jan–Mar)
                    www.cityofchicago.org/specialevents

Light Nights on the Magnificent Mile   312-642-3570
N. Michigan Ave. from the river to Oak St.
  (early Jan–late Feb)   www.themagnificentmile.com

February

Chinese New Year Parade   312-744-3315
Wentworth Ave. from Cermak Rd. to 24th St.
                    www.cityofchicago.org/specialevents

Clown Around Town   312-595-7437
Navy Pier   www.navypier.com

March

Chicago Flower and Garden Show   312-222-5086
Navy Pier   www.chicagoflower.com

St. Patrick's Day Parade   312-744-3315
Columbus Dr., from Balbo Ave. to Monroe St.
                             www.chicagostpatsparade.com

April

Chicago Antiques Fair   800-677-6278
Merchandise Mart, 300 N. Wells St.
               www.merchandisemart.com/chicagoantiques

Major League Baseball Opening Day
  Chicago Cubs   773-404-2827
  Wrigley Field   http://chicago.cubs.mlb.com
  Chicago White Sox   312-674-1000
  U.S. Cellular Field   www.chisox.com

May

ArtChicago   312-595-5100
Butler Field, Monroe St. at Lake Shore Dr.
                                          www.artchicago.com

Chicago Summer Neighborhood Festivals 312-744-3315
Various locations (May–Sept)
                    www.cityofchicago.org/specialevents

Great Chicago Places and Spaces   312-744-3370
  (architectural festival) Various locations
                    www.cityofchicago.org/specialevents

Mayor Daley's Kids and Kites Festival   312-742-1190
Monroe Harbor, Lincoln Park
                    www.cityofchicago.org/specialevents

June

Chicago Blues Festival   312-744-3370
Petrillo Bandshell, Grant Park
                    www.cityofchicago.org/specialevents

Chicago Gospel Festival   312-744-3370
Millennium Park   www.cityofchicago.org/specialevents

Old Town Art Fair   312-337-1938
W. Menomenee & N. Orleans Sts.
    www.oldtowntriangle.com

Ravinia Festival   847-266-5100
Highland Park (Jun–Sept)   www.ravinia.org

Taste of Chicago   312-744-3370
Grant Park   www.cityofchicago.org/specialevents

July

Chicago Outdoor Film Festival   312-744-3370
Butler Field, Monroe St. at Lake Shore Dr. (July–Aug)
    www.cityofchicago.org/specialevents

Fiesta del Sol   312-666-2663
Pilsen (Cermak Rd. between Throop & Morgan Sts.)
    www.fiestadelsol.org

Grant Park Music Festival   312-742-4763
Grant Park   www.grantparkmusicfestival.com

August

Bud Billiken Day Parade   312-744-3370
39th St. & King Dr.   www.cityofchicago.org/specialevents

Chicago Air & Water Show   312-744-3370
North Avenue Beach
    www.cityofchicago.org/specialevents

Viva! Chicago Latin Music Festival   312-744-3370
Grant Park   www.cityofchicago.org/specialevents

September

Celtic Fest Chicago   312-744-3370
Grant Park   www.cityofchicago.org/specialevents

Chicago Jazz Festival   312-744-3360
Petrillo Bandshell, Grant Park
    www.cityofchicago.org/specialevents

World Music Festival   312-742-1938
Various locations   www.cityofchicago.org/worldmusic

October

Chicago International Film Festival   312-425-9400
Various theaters   www.chicagofilmfestival.com

Chicago Marathon   312-904-9800
Ends at Grant Park   www.chicagomarathon.com

Halloween Happening   312-744-3370
State St., Loop   www.cityofchicago.org/specialevents

November

City of Chicago Tree-lighting Ceremony   312-744-3315
Daley Center Plaza   www.cityofchicago.org/specialevents

Day of the Dead Celebration   312-738-1503
Mexican Fine Arts Center Museum, 1852 W. 19th St.
    www.mfacmchicago.org

Mag Mile Lights Festival   312-642-3570
N. Michigan Ave.   www.themagnificentmile.com

December

New Years Eve Celebration   312-744-3370
Navy Pier   www.cityofchicago.org/specialevents

Winter Wonder Fest   312-595-7437
Navy Pier   www.navypier.com

Must Know: Practical Information

WHEN TO GO TO CHICAGO

Summer is the high tourist season, offering countless festivals and opportunities for outdoor recreation—along with hot and humid weather, and, often, rain (June, July and August are statistically the rainiest months). Fall is also popular, when crowds thin, the humidity disappears and the temperatures cool. Snow poses little threat until late November, when the Chicago winter blows in. Spring is temperamental, with conditions fluctuating from cold to warm and back again; April tends to be a rainy. Although open-air activities are limited, the winter and spring months can be a prime time to make the most of cheap hotel rates and the wide world of the indoors, from museums to malls.

Average Seasonal Temperatures in Chicago

	Jan	Apr	July	Oct
Avg. high	29°F / -2°C	58°F / 15°C	83°F / 28°C	63°F / 18°C
Avg. low	13°F / -10°C	38°F / 4°C	62°F / 17°C	42°F /6°C

PLANNING YOUR TRIP

Before you go, contact the following agencies to obtain maps and information about sightseeing, accommodations, travel packages, recreational opportunities and seasonal events.

Chicago Convention and Tourism Bureau
2301 S. Lakeshore Dr., Chicago, IL 60616
312-567-8500 or 877-244-2246; www.choosechicago.com

Chicago Office of Tourism
78 E. Washington St., Chicago, IL 60602
312-744-2400 or 877-244-2246; www.cityofchicago.org

Visitor Information Centers

Chicago Cultural Center
77 E. Randolph St.; 312-744-2400
Open year-round Mon–Fri 10am–6pm,
Sat 10am–5pm, Sun 11am–5pm.
Closed Thanksgiving Day & Dec 25.

Chicago Historic Water Tower Visitor Center
163 E. Pearson St., at Michigan Ave.
Open year-round daily 7:30am–7pm.
Closed Thanksgiving Day & Dec 25.

Sears on State Information Kiosk
2 N. State St., at Madison Ave.
Open year-round Mon-Sat 10am–6pm, Sun noon–5pm.
Closed Thanksgiving Day & Dec 25.

Web Sites

Here are some additional Web sites to help you plan your trip:
www.877chicago.com
www.metromix.com
www.themagnificentmile.com
www.chicago.il.org
www.chicagonews.com
www.chicagolandchamber.org
www.choosechicago.com

CityPass – Consider buying a CityPass booklet *($49 adults; $39 children ages 3–11; good for 7 consecutive days)*, which gives you substantially discounted admission to the following attractions: Hancock Observatory at John Hancock Center *(see Landmarks)*, the Art Institute of Chicago, the Field Museum of Natural History, the Shedd Aquarium, Adler Planetarium & Astronomy Museum, and the Museum of Science and Industry *(all museums mentioned here are described in the Museums section of this guide)*. You can purchase a CityPass at any of the participating attractions, or online at www.citypass.com.

GETTING THERE

By Air – Chicago is serviced by two international airports:

O'Hare International Airport (ORD) is one of the world's busiest airports. Located 17 miles northwest of downtown, O'Hare is served by most major domestic and international carriers *(take I-90 West to Exit 78/I-190 West; 773-686-3700; www.ohare.com)*.

Midway International Airport (MDW) has more commuter air traffic and is much less crowded than O'Hare. It's located 10 miles southwest of downtown *(take I-90 South to I-55 West to Exit 286/Cicero Ave.; 773-838-0600; www.flychicago.com)*.

Transportation Downtown – **Airport Express** offers shuttles between O'Hare, Midway, downtown hotels and North Shore suburbs year-round. Shuttles run between airports and downtown hotels daily 6am–11:30pm *(312-454-7800 or 800-654-7871; www.airportexpress.com; one passenger/one-way fare is $23 from O'Hare Airport)*. Tickets are available at Airport Express counters, located across from the baggage-claim area at both airports.

Chicago Transit Authority trains service both airports: the Blue Line runs to the Loop from O'Hare; the Orange Line train services Midway *(for schedule and fare information, see p 13)*.

Taxi service from the airports to downtown averages $30 to $35 from O'Hare and $25 to $30 from Midway.

By Train – **Amtrak** runs several lines to Chicago's Union Station, on the Near West Side *(225 S. Canal St.; 312-655-2385)*. For fares, schedule and route information, contact Amtrak *(800-872-7245 or www.amtrak.com)*.

In the News

Chicago's two main daily morning newspapers are the *Chicago Tribune* (www.chicagotribune.com) and the *Chicago Sun-Times* (www.suntimes.com). For news of what's going on when you're in town, check out the entertainment sections of the *Tribune (Friday)* and the *Sun Times (Weekend Plus)*, both published on Fridays.

A weekly alternative paper, the *Chicago Reader* (published Thu; www.chireader.com), offers a different perspective of the city as well as good coverage of the arts and nightlife. *New City* (www.newcitychicago.com) is an alternative webzine, updated daily, with special weekend editions published on Fridays. Check out the monthly *Chicago Magazine* (www.chicagomag.com) for restaurant reviews. *CS*, a free lifestyle monthly, covers nightlife, dining, fashion and shopping.

By Bus – Greyhound provides bus service to Chicago's main bus terminal, located on the Near West Side *(630 W. Harrison St.; 312-408-5980 or 800-231-2222)*. For fares, schedules and route information, contact Greyhound *(800-229-9424 or www.greyhound.com)*.

By Car – Chicago is easily accessible from a number of major highways. The Dan Ryan Expressway (I-90/I-94), the Chicago Skyway (toll road) and I-57 serve the south side while the Stevenson Expressway (I-55) offers access to the southwest. The Eisenhower Expressway (I-290), called Congress Parkway within downtown, provides the quickest route to the western suburbs. The Kennedy (I-90/94) and Edens (I-94) expressways serve the northwest and north sides respectively. Lake Shore Drive (US-41) follows the lakefront through the city to the northern suburbs. The I-294 (Tri-state Tollway) beltway rings western Chicago.

Car Rental Company	Reservations	Internet
Alamo	800-462-5266	www.alamo.com
Avis	800-230-4898	www.avis.com
Budget	800-527-0700	www.drivebudget.com
Dollar	800-800-4000	www.dollar.com
Enterprise	800-736-8222	www.enterprise.com
Hertz	800-654-3131	www.hertz.com
National	800-227-7368	www.nationalcar.com
Thrifty	800-847-4389	www.thrifty.com

GETTING AROUND

By Car – The interstates around Chicago tend to be heavily trafficked, no matter the time of day. It's not difficult to drive downtown, but parking can be a hassle; in general, you're better off walking or taking public transportation. If you do have a car, avoid driving during commuter rush hours *(weekdays 7:30am–9am & 4pm–6pm)*. Use of seat belts is required. Child safety seats are mandatory for children under 7 years of age.

Parking – Street parking can be difficult to find and public parking garages are expensive (downtown garage parking averages $7 to $17 for one to four hours). Metered street parking is available on most downtown and arterial streets; note that your vehicle will be towed if left overnight. Many streets are designated Snow Routes (indicated by red, white and blue signs); parking is not allowed on either side of these streets overnight during winter or when there are two or more inches of snow on the ground. No parking is allowed on many streets during rush hour and during specific street-cleaning days; check signs before you leave your car. Parking in some residential areas is by permit only (restricted to area residents).

By Foot – Walking is one of the best ways to explore Chicago. The Loop, River North, and the Magnificent Mile neighborhoods downtown are all easy to navigate on foot. In fact, that's the best way to take in the wonderful architecture, shopping and other attractions. Exercise caution when visiting areas in the south and west sides of Chicago.

By Public Transportation – The **Chicago Transit Authority** (**CTA**) operates an efficient and extensive network of subways, elevated trains and trolleys. For fares, schedules and route information, contact CTA *(888-968-7282 or www.transitchicago.com)*. **Pace Bus** *(847-364-7223; www.pacebus.com)* provides bus service throughout the suburbs. CTA route maps and brochures are available online, as well as at both airports, train stations and at city of Chicago information booths *(see p 10)*. Chicago's **Travel Information Hotline** is available seven days a week *(4:45am–1am)* from any Chicago area code: 836-7000.

Navy Pier Trolley

Want to take the kids to Navy Pier? Sure, you do! But it can be a hike from hotels in the Loop. Never fear. Hop aboard the free trolley that runs daily between the pier and State Street, along Grand Avenue and Illinois Street (trolley stops are marked with signs). Trolleys run about every 20 minutes *(Mon–Thu 10am–9pm, Fri & Sat 10am–11pm, Sun 10am–9pm)*.

Elevated Commuter Rail Line – *See map on inside back cover.* Known to locals as the "El," this elevated train runs through the Loop and connects all cardinal points of the city and suburbs through a system of colored lines such as the Red Line, running north-south; the Green Line, running west-south; the Blue Line, taking a west-northwest route through Wicker Park to O'Hare Airport; the Brown Line, a scenic above-ground route running north; and the Orange Line, a south-west connection to Midway Airport. Basic fare is $1.75; transfers are an extra 25¢ (for two transfers within two hours of ticket purchase). Trains operate daily 5am–1am; the Red and Blue lines operate 24 hours a day. **Visitor passes**, which allow unlimited rides on all CTA buses and trains, are available at train stations and visitor centers, or online *(1 day/$5; 2 days/$9; 3 days/$12; 5 days/$18)*.

By Taxi – Cabs are readily available at all hours in Chicago; you can hail cabs on the street, or find them outside major hotels. Riders are required to pay the fare shown on the meter, plus any tolls. The meter starts at $1.90 for the first mile, and $1.60 for each additional mile, or $2 for each minute of waiting time. Major cab companies in the city include: **Flash Cab** *(773-561-1444; www.flashcab.com)*, **Yellow Cab** *(312-829-4222; www.yellowcabchicago.com)*, and **Checker Cab** *(312-243-2537)*.

By Water – From Memorial Day to Labor Day, **Shoreline Sightseeing** *(312-222-9328; www.shorelinesightseeing.com)* operates water taxis on Lake Michigan between Navy Pier and Shedd Aquarium, and along the Chicago River from Navy Pier to the Sears Tower *(200 S. Wacker Dr.)*. Fares for a one-way ticket are $6 for adults, and $3 for children under age 12. If you're planning to go back and forth, an all-day pass is your best bet *($12 adults, $6 children under 12)*.

Chicago Greeters

First time in Chicago? Take a free tour with one of Chicago's official greeters *(312-744-8000; www.chicagogreeter.com; tours held Mon–Fri 9am–5pm)*. These savvy guides enjoy sharing their knowledge and love of the Windy City. Set aside a morning or afternoon to explore neighborhoods, parks, cultural elements, and, of course, the indispensable shops and restaurants. Tours can be one-on-one or group-oriented; "themed" tours offer jaunts for everyone from the literature buff to the sports enthusiast. Short on time? Try "InstaGreeter," the first-come, first-served mini-tour; it lets you explore downtown in an hour with a local volunteer greeter.

AREA CODES

To call between different area codes in Chicago, dial 1 + area code + seven-digit number. The same applies to local calls, even within the same area code.

Chicago (downtown): **312**
Chicago (other areas): **773**
Northern suburbs (Evanston): **847**
Southern suburbs (Oak Park): **708**
Western suburbs: **630**
Outer suburbs: **815**

Important Numbers	
Emergency (Police/Ambulance/Fire Department, 24hrs)	911
Police *(non-emergency, within Chicago)*	311
Poison Control	312-942-5969
Physician Referral	312-926-8400
Chicago Medical Society	312-670-2550
Dental Emergencies	
Chicago Dental Society	312-836-7300
24-hour Pharmacy: Walgreens	
757 N. Michigan Ave., Magnificent Mile	312-664-4000
111. S. Halsted St., Near West Side	312-463-9139
1601 N. Wells St., Old Town	312-642-4738
641 N. Clark St., South Loop	312-587-0904
Time	312-976-1616
Weather	312-976-1212

TIPS FOR SPECIAL VISITORS

Disabled Travelers – Federal law requires that businesses (including hotels and restaurants) provide access for the disabled, devices for the hearing impaired, and designated parking spaces. For further information, contact the Society for Accessible Travel and Hospitality (SATH), *(347 Fifth Ave., Suite 610, New York, NY 10016; 212-447-7284; www.sath.org)*.

All national parks have facilities for the disabled, and offer free or discounted passes. For details, contact the National Park Service *(Office of Public Inquiries, P.O. Box 37127, Room 1013, Washington, DC 20013-7127; 202-208-4747; www.nps.gov)*.

Passengers who will need assistance with train or bus travel should give advance notice to Amtrak *(800-872-7245 or 800-523-6590/TDD; www.amtrak.com)* or Greyhound *(800-752-4841 or 800-345-3109/TDD; www.greyhound.com)*. Make reservations for hand-controlled cars in advance with the rental company.

Local Lowdown – Additional detailed information about access for the disabled in the Chicago area is available from the **Mayor's Office for People with Disabilities** *(121 North LaSalle St.; Room 1104, Chicago, IL 60602; 312-744-7050; www.ci.chi.il.us/disabilities)*. They also publish a monthly newsletter called **AccessNotes**, which is available from their office.

For information about disabled access to public transportation, contact the **Chicago Transit Authority** *(312-432-7025; www.transitchicago.com)*.

Senior Citizens – Many hotels, attractions and restaurants offer discounts to visitors age 62 or older (proof of age may be required). The **AARP**, formerly the American Association of Retired Persons, offers discounts to its members *(601 E St. NW, Washington, DC 20049; 202-424-3410; www.aarp.com)*.

FOREIGN VISITORS

Visitors from outside the US can obtain information from the Chicago Convention and Tourism Bureau *(312-567-8500 or 877-244-2246; www.choosechicago.com)* or from the US embassy or consulate in their country of residence. For a complete list of American consulates and embassies abroad, visit the US State Department Bureau of Consular Affairs listing on the Internet at: *http://travel.state.gov*.

Entry Requirements – Travelers entering the United States under the Visa Waiver Program (VWP) must have a machine-readable passport. Any traveler without a machine-readable passport will be required to obtain a visa before entering the US. Citizens of VWP countries are permitted to enter the US for general business or tourist purposes for a maximum of 90 days without needing a visa. Requirements for the Visa Waiver Program can be found at the Department of State's Visa Services Web site *(http://travel.state.gov)*.

All citizens of nonparticipating countries must have a visitor's visa. Upon entry, nonresident foreign visitors must present a valid passport and round-trip transportation ticket. Canadian citizens are not required to present a passport or visa, but they must present a valid picture ID and proof of citizenship. Naturalized Canadian citizens should carry their citizenship papers.

US Customs – All articles brought into the US must be declared at the time of entry. Prohibited items include: plant material, firearms and ammunition (if not for sporting purposes), and meat or poultry products. For information, contact the US Customs Service, 1300 Pennsylvania Ave. NW, Washington, DC 20229 *(202-354-1000; www.cbp.gov)*.

Money and Currency Exchange – Visitors can exchange currency downtown in the Loop at the **Northern Trust Company** *(50 S. LaSalle St.; 312-630-6000; www.northerntrust.com; open Mon–Fri 8am–4pm)*, **World's Money Exchange, Inc.** *(203 N. LaSalle St., Suite M-1; 312-641-2151; www.wmeinc.com; open Mon–Fri 9am–5pm)*, and **American Express Travel Service** *(122 S. Michigan Ave.; 312-435-2595; www.americanexpress.com; open Mon–Fri 8:30am–5:30pm)*. American Express also has an office on the Magnificent Mile *(605 N. Michigan Ave., Suite 105; 312-435-2570; open Mon–Fri 8:30am–6pm, Sat 9am–5pm)*. **O'Hare International Airport Currency Exchange** offices *(773-686-7965)* are located on the lower level of the international terminal, at Arrivals Door A.

For cash transfers, **Western Union** *(800-325-6000; www.westernunion.com)* has agents throughout Chicago. Banks, stores, restaurants and hotels accept travelers' checks with picture identification. To report a lost or stolen credit card: **American Express** *(800-528-4800)*; **Diners Club** *(800-234-6377)*; **MasterCard** *(800-307-7309)*; **Visa** *(800-336-8472)*.

Must Know: Practical Information

Driving in the US – Visitors bearing valid driver's licenses issued by their country of residence are not required to obtain an International Driver's License. Drivers must carry vehicle registration and/or rental contract, and proof of automobile insurance at all times. Gasoline is sold by the gallon (1 gallon = 3.8 liters). Vehicles in the US are driven on the right-hand side of the road.

Electricity – Voltage in the US is 120 volts AC, 60 Hz. Foreign-made appliances may need AC adapters (available at specialty travel and electronics stores) and North American flat-blade plugs.

Taxes and Tipping – Prices displayed in Chicago do not include the Illinois sales tax of 8.75%, which is not reimbursable. It is customary to give a small gift of money—a tip—for services rendered, to waiters (15–20% of bill), porters ($1 per bag), chamber maids ($1 per day) and cab drivers (15% of fare).

Time Zone – Chicago is in the **Central Time** (CT) zone, one hour behind New York City and six hours behind Greenwich Mean Time.

Measurement Equivalents

Degrees Fahrenheit	95°	86°	77°	68°	59°	50°	41°	32°	23°	14°
Degrees Celsius	35°	30°	25°	20°	15°	10°	5°	0°	-5°	-10°

1 inch = 2.54 centimeters   1 foot = 30.5 centimeters
1 mile = 1.6 kilometers   1 pound = 0.45 kilograms
1 quart = 0.9 liters   1 gallon = 3.8 liters

ACCOMMODATIONS

For a list of suggested accommodations, see Must Stay. An area visitors' guide including lodging directory is available free-of-charge from the Chicago Convention and Visitors Bureau *(p 10)*.

Hotel Reservation Services

At Home Inn Chicago – 312-640-1050 or 800-375-7084. www.athomeinn chicago.com. Focuses on city-style B&B accommodations.

Hot Rooms – 773-468-7666. www.hotrooms.com.

Hotel Reservations Network – 800-964-6835. www.hoteldiscounts.com.

Hotels.com – 800-246-8357. www.hotels.com.

Illinois Hotel & Lodging Association – 877-456-3446. www.stayillinois.com.

Hostels

A no-frills, inexpensive alternative to hotels, hostels are a great choice for budget travelers. Prices average $17 to $35 per night for a dorm-style room.

Chicago International Hostel – 6318 N. Winthrop Ave., Lakeview. 773-262-1011. www.chicagointernationalhostel.com.

Hostelling International-Chicago – 24 E. Congress Pkwy. at Wabash St., in the Loop. 312-360-0300. www.hichicago.org.

Chicago Summer Hostel – Open June–Sept. 731 S. Plymouth Ct. at Polk St., in the South Loop. 773-327-5350 (summer); 312-360-0300 (off season). www.hiayh.org.

Major hotel and motel chains with locations in Chicago include:

Property	Contact	Web site
Best Western	800-780-7234	www.bestwestern.com
Comfort, Clarion & Quality Inns	877-424-6423	www.choicehotels.com
Days Inn	800-329-7466	www.daysinn.com
Hilton	800-774-1500	www.hilton.com
Holiday Inn	800-465-4329	www.holiday-inn.com
Hyatt	800-233-1234	www.hyatt.com
ITT Sheraton	888-625-5144	www.sheraton.com
Marriott	888-236-2427	www.marriott.com
Omni	800-843-6664	www.omnihotels.com
Radisson	888-201-1718	www.radisson.com
Ramada	800-228-2828	www.ramada.com
Westin	888-625-5144	www.westin.com

SPECTATOR SPORTS

Chicago's major professional sports teams are listed below. *For more information about the sports scene in Chicago, check online at: www.chicagosports.com.*

Sport/Team	Season	Venue	Phone	Web site
Baseball/ Chicago Cubs (National League)	Apr–Oct	Wrigley Field	773-404-2827	http://chicago.cubs.mlb.com
Baseball/ Chicago White Sox (American League)	Apr–Oct	U.S. Cellular Field	312-674-1000	www.chisox.com
Basketball/ Chicago Bulls	Nov–Apr	United Center	312-455-4500	www.nba.com/bulls
Football/ Chicago Bears	Sept–Dec	Soldier Field	847-615-2327	www.chicagobears.com
Hockey (NHL) /Chicago Blackhawks	Oct–Apr	United Center	312-455-4500	www.chicagoblackhawks.com
Hockey (AHL) /Chicago Wolves	Oct–Apr	Allstate Arena	800-843-9658	www.chicagowolves.com
Soccer/ Chicago Fire	Mar–Oct	Soldier Field	888-657-3473	www.chicago.fire.mlsnet.com

City of Big Shoulders: Chicago, Illinois

THE CITY OF CHICAGO.

Chicago was never destined to be a great city; the odds, from the get-go, were stacked against it. But mud, fire, labor unrest, gangsters, shady politics and the Cubs only seem to have strengthened Chicago's character. Settled in 1779 by Jean-Baptiste Point du Sable on a swampy riverbank, Chicago takes its name from the native Potawatomi word She-caw-gu, meaning "stinking onion"— a reference to the garlic that grew wild in the area.

Chicago Grows Up – By 1837, when the city was incorporated, Chicago had a population of a mere 4,000; it would top 300,000 by 1871 and 1.5 million at the turn of the 20C—but not without a lot of hard work. The quagmire on which the city was built thwarted road and building construction and contributed to the spread of disease. In the 1850s, Chicago tardily began installing sewers; lines were placed at street level and the streets and structures raised around them. Storm overflow and sewage dumped into the Chicago River, and to protect drinking water and prevent cholera, a scheme was hatched to reverse the river's flow away from the lake. By 1900 engineers finally succeeded in permanently reversing the river's flow, much to the chagrin of communities downstream.

Despite the setbacks, Chicago's central location between the Mississippi River and the Great Lakes became increasingly strategic as the hub of transportation, commerce and industry in an expanding America. Lumber, grain and livestock funneled through Chicago in monumental quantities. City fathers frantically constructed tunnels, bridges and roads to accommodate the busy metropolis, and Irish and German laborers arrived in droves to do the work.

In October 1871, the **Great Chicago Fire** broke out, burning for three days and destroying the central city. Rebuilding began immediately and growth continued unabated; the population tripled in the decade following the fire. In spite of crowding, poor sanitation and grueling working conditions, Chicago rose above the miasma of its stockyards and steel mills. After 1880, the central city grew tall on the talents of a coterie of architects who pioneered the Chicago school of architecture.

Carl Sandburg's Chicago

"Hog Butcher for the World,
Tool Maker, Stacker of Wheat,
Player with Railroads and the Nation's Freight Handler:
Stormy, husky, brawling,
City of the Big Shoulders . . ."
　　　Carl Sandburg, 1916, *"Chicago"*

Nearly 100,000 immigrants were arriving weekly in the 1880s, hoping to find work in this industrial promised land. Not for long, however, could they endure the conditions and low wages forced upon them. Labor unrest brewed strikes and mayhem, including the infamous **Haymarket Riot** of 1886, where seven policemen were killed and eight workers were unjustly convicted of murder.

By the 1890s, elite residents had leisure time and money enough to establish cultural institutions. The crowning achievement would be the staging of the **World's Columbian Exposition** *(see p 58)* in 1893 on the South Side lakefront. A showcase of Neoclassical architecture and modern technology, the fair established Chicago as a world-class city.

Bootleggers and Power Brokers – The Roaring Twenties left a permanent scar, as bootlegging gangsters, **Al Capone** foremost among them, committed hundreds of murders in their attempts to control the illegal liquor business. Another mob, of sorts, came into its own when the Democratic Machine hit its stride under Richard J. Daley, "Hizzoner da Mare," in 1955. His "City that Works" did so because the mayor knew how to exchange influence to get things done. Daley died in 1976, taking the power with him. When Harold Washington, the city's first black mayor, triumphantly took office in 1983, many looked forward to a new chapter. The book closed, however, with Washington's untimely death in office four years later.

Waiting in the wings, Richard M. Daley rose to assume his father's throne; he has emerged as a no-nonsense mayor of moderation.

Of today's 2.9 million Chicagoans, nearly 35 percent are African American, 26 percent Hispanic and over 4 percent Asian. And the historic mix of Polish, German, Irish, Central European, Italian and Greek still spices the multicultural stew, giving Chicago a texture, a world view and an accent all its own. And the Cubs? Well, just wait 'til next year.

Chicago Fast Facts and Firsts

- Chicago covers 228 square miles.
- The city is home to 2.9 million people.
- Chicago invented the zipper, Twinkies, and the smoke-filled room.
- Chicago birthed the first skyscraper and the first controlled atomic reaction.
- In 2004 alone, 64 movies and TV shows were filmed in Chicago.
- Lake Michigan is the fifth-largest body of fresh water in the world.
- The Chicago Board of Trade is the world's oldest and largest futures exchange.

Chicago is a city of neighborhoods—urban, busy, crowded, yes, but also tree-lined and intimate. From the Far South Side, up through Bronzeville and Chinatown, around Pilsen, and finally through the Loop into the upscale neighborhoods of the Magnificent Mile and the Gold Coast, the patchwork that is Chicago offers something new, literally, around each corner.

The Loop★★★

See map on inside front cover.

Looming large along the lakefront, south of the Chicago River, the city's busy Loop has been fertile ground for architectural innovation since the fire in 1871 destroyed the downtown business district. Named for the elevated tracks that girdle them, these blocks bustle with workday energy as Chicagoans transact their daily business in an array of office towers that catalogs the city's growth skyward since the 19C. **State Street**★ has recently renewed its traditional role as a busy shopping corridor *(see Must Shop)*, and in the evenings, the Loop offers a selection of theater, music and dining experiences.

In the Loop

Auditorium Building★★★

430 S. Michigan Ave. 312-431-2389, ext. 0. www.auditoriumtheatre.org. Theater may be visited by guided tour only; reservations required; call ahead for times.

This solid cornerstone of the Loop's east side launched the careers of renowned architects Louis Sullivan and Dankmar Adler, as well as a young draftsman named Frank Lloyd Wright *(see p 95)*. Completed in 1889, it housed a hotel, an office tower and a theater and was Chicago's tallest building at the time. The spectacular theater remains an acoustic marvel; enter the lobby on Congress Parkway to see some of Sullivan's intri-

cate designs. Better yet, reserve tickets for one of the dance or musical theater productions held here between November and June.

Looping the Loop

Most Chicagoans agree that the best way to explore the Loop is on foot. However, the city offers some fun alternative methods of getting around this neighborhood:

By Boat – The best way to see Chicago's skyscrapers is from the river. Cruises depart from the docks on both sides of the Michigan Avenue Bridge, near the **Riverwalk**★, a great place for a stroll in nice weather. *For more information on river tours, see p 38.*

By the "L" – Take the elevated Brown Line (Ravenswood) to circle the Loop.

By Train – A free 40-minute train tour affords the same views as the "L" *(offered on a first-come, first-served basis May–Sept, Sat 11:35am & 12:55pm).*

Carson Pirie Scott & Company★★★

1 S. State St. 312-641-7000. www.carsons.com. Open year-round Mon–Fri 9:45am–8pm (opens at 9am Tue & Wed), Sat 6am–6pm, Sun 11am–6pm; hours vary seasonally. Closed Easter Sunday, Thanksgiving Day & Dec 25.

Carson's is State Street's *other* historic department store (after Marshall Field). Architect Louis Sullivan's incredible skill with ornament is evident in the cast iron that embroiders the building's rounded front corner. Indeed, this 1899 structure represents the height of Sullivan's ornamental genius.

Chicago Cultural Center★★

78 E. Washington St. 312-744-6630. www.cityofchicago.org/tour/culturalcenter. Open year-round Mon–Thu 10am–7pm, Fri 10am–6pm, Sat 10am–5pm, Sun 11am–5pm. Closed Thanksgiving Day & Dec 25.

This marvelous Neoclassical palace served as the city's first library when it was completed in 1897. Today it functions as an all-purpose exhibition, arts and music center, and also houses the **Chicago Office of Tourism Visitor Information Center** *(312-744-2400)*.

Enter from Washington Street and ascend the grand staircase to **Preston-Bradley Hall★** (note the Tiffany stained-glass dome), where free concerts are offered Monday through Friday at 12:15pm and on Sunday at 3pm.

Public Sculpture in the Loop

The Bowman and the Spearman Ivan Mestrovic	Grant Park, Grand Entrance
Chicago Stock Exchange Arch Dankmar Adler and Louis Sullivan	Art Institute, Columbus Dr. entrance
Dawn Shadows Louise Nevelson	Madison Plaza
Flamingo Alexander Calder	Federal Center Plaza
Four Seasons Marc Chagall	First National Bank Plaza
Miró's Chicago Joan Miró	Washington St., next to Chicago Temple
Monument with Standing Beast Jean Dubuffet	James R. Thompson Center Plaza
The Seated Lincoln Augustus Saint-Gaudens	Grant Park, Court of Presidents
Untitled Pablo Picasso	Daley Center Plaza

Federal Center★★

On Dearborn St., between Adams St. & Jackson Blvd.

Completed in 1974, this three-building complex is a wonderful example of the steel-and-glass International style for which architect Ludwig Mies van der Rohe became so famous. Though unadorned, its beauty depends on its perfect proportions. The restrained buildings form a perfect frame for Alexander Calder's fiery, flamboyant sculpture **Flamingo** (1973).

James R. Thompson Center★★

Bounded by Clark, LaSalle, Randolph & Lake Sts.

Architectural "bad boy" Helmut Jahn, known for bucking accepted trends, designed this State of Illinois facility to resemble the domes you're used to seeing on government buildings. Though quirky, the shape makes possible the soaring **atrium**★, which rises the full 17 stories and encloses open office floors. Catch a snack at the lower-level food court and enjoy the constantly changing play of light and shadow that filters into the airy space. **Monument with Standing Beast**, a curvaceous fiberglass sculpture by Jean Dubuffet, adorns the plaza.

> **Touring Tip**
>
> For a good panorama of the north side of the river, venture to the corner of Clark Street and Wacker Drive. That massive pile to the left is the **Merchandise Mart**, all 4.1 million square feet of it *(see Must Shop)*. To the right, the corncob towers of Marina City stand out, and just east of them, the IBM Building. Below it, the *Sun-Times* headquarters and printing press once stood; it was demolished in 2004 to make way for the new Trump Tower, scheduled for completion in 2008.

Richard J. Daley Center★★

Bounded by Washington, Clark, Randolph & Dearborn Sts.

The Daley Center is probably best known for its plaza, where Picasso's fantastic steel creature holds court. Chicagoans shuddered at first, but the beast may

now be as famous (and beloved) as "Hizzoner da Mare" himself, who governed the city from 1955 to 1976. Housing courtrooms and offices, this fine example of the International style was completed in 1965. Seasonal festivities and a summertime farmers' market take place under the Picasso.

Chicago Board of Trade Building★

141 W. Jackson Blvd. 312-435-3590. www.cbot.com.

Hog futures, anyone? The Board of Trade was founded in 1848 to regulate trade of the Midwest's bountiful agricultural commodities. This outstanding Art Deco skyscraper (1930, Holabird & Root) testifies to that abundance, anchoring the south end of the LaSalle Street financial district. Ceres, the goddess of the harvest, gazes down from high atop the building's soaring roof. Today all the action takes place inside on the 60,000-square-foot trading floors, where frenetic traders in brightly colored jackets buy and sell stock options and commodities.

Scraping the Sky

A talented and energetic group of architects—William Le Baron Jenney, Louis Sullivan, William Holabird, Martin Roche, Daniel Burnham, John Wellborn Root and others—rebuilt Chicago after the 1871 fire. Within a year, 10,000 new buildings rose up at a cost of $45 million. By 1890 the booming population needed more offices. With no place to go but up, Chicago architects and engineers created the skyscraper. In traditional masonry construction, thick walls support the weight of the building. Architect William Le Baron Jenney reversed the formula by hanging "curtain" walls on a skeletal steel frame, allowing buildings to grow taller. Based on this steel-frame construction, Jenney's 1884 nine-story Home Insurance Building, now demolished, is considered the first modern "skyscraper." Engineers mastered ways to anchor tall buildings in Chicago's swampy soil and to reduce the effects of high winds. Improvements to the elevator and the telephone made vertical height practical. Thus, the **Chicago school** of architecture was born, recognized as the first significant new movement in architecture since the Italian High Renaissance.

You can still glimpse the scale of 19C Chicago in the 16-story **Monadnock Building**★★ *(53 W. Jackson Blvd.),* the tallest masonry structure in Chicago; the 1895 **Reliance Building**★★ *(32 N. State St.),* now reincarnated as the Hotel Burnham *(see Must Stay);* the **Marquette Building**★★ *(140 S. Dearborn St.),* whose lobby features a stunning Tiffany glass **mosaic**★ illustrating the journeys of French explorer Jacques Marquette; and the **Rookery**★★ *(southeast corner of LaSalle & Adams Sts.),* named for the pigeons who invaded a temporary city hall erected here in 1871. Once your eye becomes familiar with the style, you'll spot many others.

Marshall Field's★

*111 N. State St. 312-781-1000.
www.fields.com. Open year-round Mon–
Fri 9am–8pm, Sun 11am–6pm. Closed
major holidays.*

This grand old department store
occupies an entire block at the
north end of fabled State Street. It
was completed in stages between
1892 and 1914 by D.H. Burnham &
Co., and its richly embellished
corner clock remains a Chicago
icon. The interior features over a
million square feet of retail space
and a lovely Tiffany favrile dome. If
you're in town around the holidays,
take in Marshall Field's legendary
decorated windows and have lunch
under the 45-foot Christmas tree in
the Walnut Room restaurant.

Food at Field's

Marshall Field is a great place to go when you get hungry; the department store has a
restaurant for every taste. On the 7th floor, the white-tablecloth **Walnut Room** *(312-
781-3125)* conjures up bygone days when genteel gloved and hatted ladies lunched in
the middle of their busy shopping day. You'll find a lighter lunch and soda-fountain
desserts at the **Frango Café** *(312-781-2945)*, where you can also buy Chicago's Frango
mints, though Field's famous candies are no longer made here. **Seven on State** *(312-
781-3693)* serves grilled Thai shrimp, ham crêpes and other upscale dishes in a sleek
food-court setting. For burgers and pub fare, try **Infield's**, where nonshoppers can
catch up on their sports news.

State Street★

The song that made State Street—"that great street"—famous ("Chicago"
by Fred Fisher) dates back to 1922, when merchants liked to call the intersec-
tion at State and Madison streets the "World's Busiest Corner." True or not,
everybody crowded State Street in those days: shoppers, movie and theatergoers, office workers. But State Street had been great since the 1860s when
real-estate magnate Potter Palmer bought a stretch of the muddy, narrow
byway. He convinced the city council to widen it, replaced rundown shacks
with the elegant Palmer House Hotel, and lured Field, Leiter and Company
from Lake Street by building them a new department store. Suddenly, State
Street was *the* place to be. Though all was destroyed by the 1871 fire, the
street came back with a vengeance. As you stroll the blocks between Wacker
and Congress, look for signs recounting more State Street history *(or visit
www.greaterstatestreet.com).*

Magnificent Mile★★★

The Champs Elysées of Chicago, this promenade along **North Michigan Avenue**, from the Chicago River north to Oak Street, is the city's most prestigious thoroughfare, blooming with plantings in the summer and twinkling with holiday lights all winter. Lined with exclusive boutiques and large retail stores, luxury hotels and premier residential and office high rises, the "Boul Mich" has come a long way from its beginnings as an ordinary city street.

Its most distinctive relics survived the Great Fire in 1871: the bizarre 1869 **Water Tower**★ still stands toward the north end at Chicago Avenue *(see Landmarks)*. The opening of the **Michigan Avenue Bridge**★ *(Wacker Dr. & N. Michigan Ave.)* joined the north and south sides of the city in 1920, igniting an incredible building boom that spawned most of the original landmarks on the avenue. The **John Hancock Center**★★★ *(see Landmarks)* and **Water Tower Place**★ *(no. 835)* ushered in a new era of skyscrapers and retailing in the early 1970s when Michigan Avenue displaced State Street as the city's shopping corridor *(see Must Shop)*.

Streeterville★

Between the lake and North Michigan Avenue, **Streeterville** was settled in the 1880s by Capt. George Streeter, who declared it the "District of Lake Michigan," separate from the city of Chicago. Bounded on the south by the Chicago River, the area is the home of Northwestern University's Chicago campus and the residential towers at **860-880 North Lake Shore Drive**★★, which established the high-rise influence of modern architect Ludwig Mies van der Rohe in the early 1950s. To the east lies **Navy Pier**★★ *(see Musts for Fun and Musts for Kids)*.

Along the Boulevard

Sights below are arranged in geographical order, from south to north. See map, p28–29.

Wrigley Building★★

400-410 N. Michigan Ave.

Set majestically on the north side of the river, this sparkling structure was built in two stages (30 stories to the south in 1920 and 21 to the north in 1924, both designed by Graham, Anderson, Probst & White). The white terra-cotta exterior, its six subtle shades chosen to add more luster at the top, is particularly stunning when it's lit up at night.

Tribune Tower★★

435 N. Michigan Ave.

Corporate headquarters of the Tribune Company's vast empire, this soaring tower (Hood & Howells), built in 1925, is a true "cathedral of commerce." Besides its dramatic Gothic style, the "Trib Tower" is known for the fragments and stones from the world's famous structures and sites that were collected by *Tribune* correspondents and embedded in its exterior walls. Look closely to find stones from the Berlin Wall, Omaha Beach, the Taj Mahal and 117 others.

InterContinental Chicago★

505 N. Michigan Ave. 312-944-4100.
www.interconti.com. See Must Stay.

The gold-leaf dome atop this 41-story building was a popular design among the Shriners, a Masonic fraternity, for whom the building was constructed as an athletic club in 1929. Step through its heavy bronze doors into a quasi-Eastern fantasia of design. Today's modern hotel (opened in 1990) retains the club's opulent Oriental decoration and its Olympic-size swimming pool on the 14th floor.

Museum of Contemporary Art ★ –

220 E. Chicago Ave.
See Museums.

American Girl Place –

111 E. Chicago Ave. See Musts for Kids.

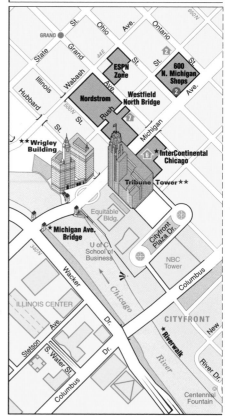

MAGNIFICENT MILE

Hotels

1. Allerton Crowne Plaza
2. Chicago's Lenox Suites Hotel
3. The Drake Hotel
4. Fitzpatrick Chicago
5. Four Seasons
6. InterContinental Chicago
7. Le Meridien
8. Millennium Knickerbocker Hotel
9. The Peninsula Chicago
10. The Raphael
11. Red Roof Inn
12. Seneca Hotel
13. Sofitel Chicago Water Tower
14. Talbott Hotel
15. The Tremont Hotel
16. W Chicago Lakeshore
17. The Whitehall Hotel

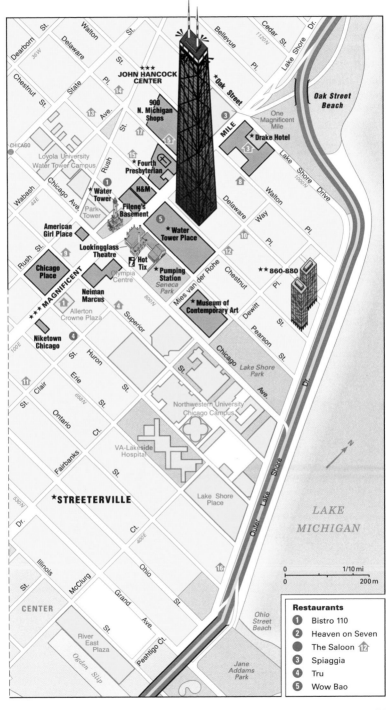

★★★ JOHN HANCOCK CENTER

★Oak Street

MILE

One Magnificent Mile

Oak Street Beach

900 N. Michigan Shops

★Drake Hotel

CHICAGO

Loyola University Water Tower Campus

★Fourth Presbyterian

H&M

★Water Tower

Park Tower

Filene's Basement

American Girl Place

Lookingglass Theatre

Hot Tix

Olympia Centre

★Water Tower Place

★Pumping Station

Seneca Park

★★860-880

Chicago Place

MAGNIFICENT

Neiman Marcus

Allerton Crowne Plaza

★Museum of Contemporary Art

Mies van der Rohe

★★★ Niketown Chicago

Northwestern University Chicago Campus

Lake Shore Park

VA-Lakeside Hospital

Lake Shore Place

★STREETERVILLE

LAKE MICHIGAN

CENTER

River East Plaza

Ogden Slip

Ohio Street Beach

Jane Addams Park

0 — 1/10 mi
0 — 200 m

Restaurants

1	Bistro 110
2	Heaven on Seven
●	The Saloon
3	Spiaggia
4	Tru
5	Wow Bao

Neighborhoods

Fourth Presbyterian Church★

N. Michigan Ave. at Delaware Pl. 312-787-4570. www.fourthchurch.org. Open year-round daily 9am–5pm. Closed major holidays.

Duck into this quiet sanctuary to escape Michigan Avenue's hustle and bustle. Dedicated in 1914, the church is an elegant reminder of Michigan Avenue's bygone character. A blend of French and English Gothic styles, the church seats 1,500 people and is softly lit by stunning medieval-style stained-glass windows. Controversy swirls today around the high-rise condominiums planned for the airspace above this lovely place of worship.

Oak Street★ – *Between N. Michigan Ave. & Rush St. See Must Shop.*

The Drake Hotel★

140 E. Walton St. 312-787-2200. www.thedrakehotel.com. See Must Stay.

Grand dame of Chicago's luxury hotels, the Drake retains its 1920s atmosphere. Occupying a prominent spot at the top of Michigan Avenue, it overlooks Oak Street Beach and Lake Shore Drive. Step up into the dignified lobby to admire the plush red-velvet wall coverings, the wooden caisson ceiling and the elegant Palm Court. Be sure to stay for tea.

High Tea at the Drake

Now, this is the life: sipping Darjeeling tea amid lush plantings and silken furniture, nibbling on tiny sandwiches, scones and clotted cream. If the sun is over the yardarm, tipple a Tea-Time-Tini, all to the dulcet tones of the harp. The Drake Hotel serves a British-style high tea each afternoon in its elegant **Palm Court** *(daily 1:30pm–5pm; reservations recommended; 312-787-2200; www.thedrakehotel.com)*. It may be just the ticket for a late afternoon pick-me-up . . . or perhaps you just like tiny sandwiches.

The Magnificent Mile Lights Festival

Chicagoans love festivals and fireworks, and not just in the summer. Michigan Avenue dresses up for the holidays on the weekend before Thanksgiving with the Magnificent Mile Lights Festival. A Saturday of music, ice carving and performances up and down the avenue culminates with the illumination of more than a million twinkling lights and a parade led by Mickey Mouse. Fireworks over the Chicago River end the evening with a bang. Stores are open late if you want to get a jump on your holiday shopping. *For more information, check online at www.themagnificentmile.com.*

River North★★

Between the Chicago River & North Branch, and Oak St. & Michigan Ave.
www.rivernorthassociation.com.

Bounded on the west and south by the Chicago River, this neighborhood includes Wolf Point at the river's bend, one of Chicago oldest areas of settlement. Early industries and shantytowns established themselves along the river, while the northeast corner sprouted mansions and cathedrals. Over the decades, working class, immigrant, bohemian and wealthy residents staked claims around this neighborhood, which now claims many of the city's best galleries, restaurants and nightclubs.

Gallery Hopping in River North

The **River North Gallery District** *(see Must Shop)* spans an eight-square-block area in River North. You'll find dozens of galleries here exhibiting an array of styles and media. On certain Friday evenings each month *(5pm–8pm)*, the galleries open their new shows *(for schedules, check online at www.chicagogallerynews.com or pick up a free copy of Chicago Gallery News)*.

Newberry Library★★

60 W. Walton St. 312-943-9090. www.newberry.org. Reading rooms open year-round. Tue–Thu 10am–6pm, Fri–Sat 9am–5pm. Closed Sun & major holidays.

Want to look up your family tree? This respected institution, completed in 1893, ranks among the top independent research libraries in the country for genealogists and scholars in the humanities. Rotating exhibits—on such diverse topics as *Alice in Wonderland* and King Arthur—draw heavily on the library's collections and offer the general public an opportunity to sample the rare book, manuscript and map treasures. A look around the lobby will give you a good sense of the building's grandeur.

Marina City★

300 N. State St.

From the river's edge rise the twin "corncob" towers of Bertrand Goldberg's experimental urban community. Revolutionary when conceived in 1959, the complex, which includes apartments as well as entertainment and services, was an attempt to encourage young professionals to settle in the city. The towers' cast-concrete construction and rippling surfaces contrast dramatically with the "glass boxes" so popular at the time.

Merchandise Mart – *300 N. Wells St.*
See Must Shop.

Gold Coast★

Between Oak St. & North Ave., and extending west from the lake to LaSalle St.

This slice of Chicago's lakefront has been home to the city's well-to-do for over a century. While all but a few of the mansions that once lined Lake Shore Drive have been demolished, you can still step back a century with a walk along State Parkway and landmark **Astor Street★★**, where quaint Victorian town houses and graystones occupy tiny, beautifully cultivated lots.

Chicago Architecture Foundation Tours

Throughout the year, knowledgeable docents at the Chicago Architecture Foundation (CAF) lead 78 different neighborhood walks. And lest you feel timid about architecture, fear not. These excellent tours make stone and steel come alive, and you'll meet some of Chicago's most interesting characters along the way. For schedules and fees, contact CAF headquarters at the **ArchiCenter** *(224 S. Michigan Ave.; 312-922-3432, ext. 240; www.architecture.org).*

Charnley-Persky House★

1365 Astor St., at Schiller St. 312-573-0105. www.sah.org. Visit by one-hour guided tour only year-round Wed at noon (free). Sat tours offered Apr–Nov 10am & 1pm, Dec–Mar 10am ($5).

With its plain brick and limestone facade and horizontal form, the Charnley-Persky House stands out amid the Victorian residential architecture that was popular at the turn of the century. Architect Louis Sullivan and Frank Lloyd Wright—a young draftsman at the time—designed the house in 1892 for lumberman James Charnley. Inside, 11 rooms surround a central skylit staircase; the kitchen is located in the narrow basement.

Oak Street Beach – *Lake Shore Dr. at Oak St. See Outdoor Fun.*

Old Town★

Bounded by Division, Halsted & LaSalle Sts., and Armitage Ave.

Working-class German families settled this area in the 1840s and 50s, and by 1900, North Avenue—the German Broadway—was alive with shops, bakeries, taverns and delicatessens. In the early 20C, as the Germans moved north, the neighborhood fell into disrepair. It remained largely so until the low rents began to attract an artistic clientele in the mid-19C. In 1959 **The Second City** comedy improv theater *(see Nightlife)* took root here. The area's funky reputation lingered into the 1990s, now having all but disappeared as the 21C ushered in a retail and residential building boom in Old Town and environs. Take a walk through **Old Town Triangle** *(bounded roughly by North & Lincoln Aves.)* to get a sense of the way people lived in the 1800s.

Menomonee Street★

The 300 block of this quaint street evokes the essence of historic Old Town. Nine cottages on its south side, **nos. 325-345**, are good examples of the small wooden cottages originally built here; they could be erected in no time using "balloon framing." This Chicago building innovation was in part accountable for the rapid growth and combustibility of the city. The tiny house at **no. 216** is a rare example of a fire-relief shanty, one of 5,200 one-room dwellings built with funds donated by the Chicago Fire Relief and Aid Society for families left homeless by the fire.

Chicago Historical Society★ – *1600 North Ave. See Museums.*

Old Town Art Fair

A neighborhood fund-raising initiative begun in 1947 evolved into the Old Town Art Fair, which today draws thousands of art lovers to the area just north of North Avenue the second weekend in June. The premier fair features more than 250 artists, a silent jewelry auction, food, music and more *($5 donation requested). For more information, contact the Old Town Triangle Association: 312-337-1938 or www.oldtowntriangle.com.*

Pilsen

Southwest of downtown, from the Chicago River west to the city limits.

Pilsen started out in the 19C as the largest settlement of Bohemian immigrants in the country. Over the years, Germans, Irish, Polish and Lithuanians passed through here, and today Pilsen forms the core of Chicago's enormous Hispanic population. The neighborhood, which centers on Halsted and 18th streets, also attracts artists, who open their studios in late September or early October each year for the **Pilsen East Artists Open House** *(312-738-8000)*. You can see much of Pilsen's art, however—in the form of large, colorful murals—on any excursion down 18th Street. Taquerias, markets and shops line the street as well; stop by **Restaurante Nuevo Leon** *(1515 W. 18th St.; 312-421-1517)* for a delicious traditional Mexican meal served in a family atmosphere. In late July, the **Fiesta del Sol** livens up the blocks from Throop to Morgan streets with outdoor music, food and fun *(312-666-2663; www.fiestadelsol.org)*.

Mexican Fine Arts Center Museum – *1852 W. 19th St. See Museums.*

Chicago has no towering monuments or hallowed spaces. This is a practical city where the most important landmarks are working buildings in busy neighborhoods. Indeed, the city of Chicago has conferred "landmark status" on 203 individual sites and 36 districts, from the Black Metropolis-Bronzeville District on the South Side to the Uptown Theater on the north. Besides these literal landmarks, however, certain icons say "Chicago" around the world.

John Hancock Center★★★

875 N. Michigan Ave.

Muscular and monumental, nothing says Chicago like the profile of "Big John." Built in 1969 (Skidmore, Owings & Merrill), the 100-story tower is a city unto itself, its 2.8 million square feet housing retail, restaurant, office and residential space. These homes are the highest in the world—for now, anyway. They're soon to be "trumped" by Trump Tower, which, when it opens in 2008 on the north bank of the Chicago River, will offer condos that are even higher.

The Hancock tower's tapering frame is crisscrossed by brawny braces, which eliminate the need for inner support beams, greatly enlarging the usable space inside. Made of some 46,000 tons of steel, the building can easily withstand gravity and wind. It's lovely at night, when a band of lights girdles the heights of the building in festive holiday color or plain bright white.

Walk around to the west side of the building's base and follow the wide steps down into a large sunken plaza framing colorful planters and a waterfall. From the plaza you'll have interesting views of the surrounding Mag Mile skyscrapers and a sheltered place to soak up the sun and enjoy a cup of coffee.

High-altitude Dining: Signature Room at the 95th

For breathtaking views of the lake and Navy Pier, with food to match, take the elevator up to the Signature Room on the 95th floor *(312-787-9596; www.signature room.com)*. The lavish lunch buffet (or you can order off the menu) is a treat, and dinnertime offerings include well-prepared seafood and hearty meat dishes. If you're not up for an expensive dinner, go up one floor to the **Signature Lounge at the 96th** for 360-degree panoramas, a bit of jazz and a specialty martini. Or perhaps a nightcap and dessert. Dress is "upscale casual."

The Hancock Observatory

On the 94th floor of the John Hancock Center. 312-751-3680 or 888-875-8439. www.hancock-observatory.com. Open daily 9am–11pm (last ticket sold at 10:45pm). $9.50 adults, $6 children (free for children under age 4).

During the 39 seconds that the elevator takes to ascend to the 94th floor, your ears will pop and your stomach will drop. Once there, however, the panoramic **views**★★★ of lake and landscape in every direction are well worth the ride. On a clear day, you'll see four states: Illinois, Indiana, Wisconsin and Michigan, and, of
course, the watery expanse of Lake Michigan that stretches east and north. The open-air **Skywalk**, the highest balcony in America, allows visitors to experience the weather a thousand feet up. Other attractions, such as a history wall, recorded tours and talking telescopes are fun and informative, but let's face it—it's the view that counts!

Sears Tower★★★

233 S. Wacker Dr.

Tallest building in the world for over 20 years, this 110-story feat of engineering cuts an unmistakable profile on the city's skyline. At the time of its construction, from 1968 to 1974, the city did not require a zoning variance for the tower, allowing it to rise to an unsurpassed height of 1,450 feet. Since 1996, the tower has been twice topped as world's tallest building; first by the Petronas Towers in Kuala Lumpur, Malaysia, and in 2003 by Taipei 101 in Taipei, Taiwan. The Sears Tower still holds the title of world's tallest building to the tips of its antennae, and it remains—so far—the tallest building in the US.

It may also be the deepest. Designed by Skidmore, Owings & Merrill, one of the most influential architectural firms of the 20C, the Sears Tower is composed of nine rectangular tubes resting on more than 100 steel and concrete caissons anchored into the bedrock hundreds of feet below ground. These 75-foot-high bundled tubes provide maximum resistance to high winds; two tubes end at the 50th floor, two at the 66th floor, and three more at the 90th floor. Clad in black aluminum and bronze-tinted glass, the tower's structural skeleton required more than 75,000 tons of steel. Check out the barrel-vaulted entrance on Wacker Drive, where sculptor Alexander Calder's mobile **The Universe**, a collection of brightly colored forms, turns and twirls.

Tower Facts

- Even in high wind, the top of the Sears Tower never sways more than six inches.

- The tower weighs in at 222,500 tons, and it's covered by 28 acres of black aluminum.

Skydeck

Enter on Jackson Blvd., between Wacker Dr. & Franklin St. 312-875-9696. www.theskydeck.com. Open May–Sept 10am–10pm. Rest of the year 10am–8pm. $9.95 adults, $6.95 children.

New elevators blast off to the top of the Sears Tower at 1,600 feet per minute. When you land on the Skydeck, 103 stories up, an awesome **view**★★★ (on a clear day) for 50 miles around greets you. Interactive exhibits, telescopes and kid-level views help you pick out sites 1,353 feet below.

Tall Tales

If size matters to you, here's how the Sears Tower and "Big John" stack up:

	Sears	John Hancock
Height	1,450 feet without antennas	1,127 feet
Stories	110	100
Weight	222,500 tons	192,000 tons
Square feet	4.5 million	2.8 million
Elevators	103	50
Top elevator speed	1,600 feet per minute	1,800 feet per minute
Number of windows	16,100	11,459
Steps to the top	2,232	1,632

Buckingham Fountain★★ – *Columbus Dr., at Congress Pkwy. in Grant Park. See Parks and Gardens.*

Navy Pier★★ – *600 E. Grand Ave., at Lake Michigan. See Musts for Fun and Musts for Kids.*

Chicago's Watermark

Of course, the biggest landmark (watermark, really) in the city spreads out from its doorstep over 22,000 square miles. That would be **Lake Michigan**, and it is indeed an awe-inspiring sight. The name comes from an Algonquian word meaning "big lake," but actually, Michigan is but the third-largest of the five Great Lakes and the only one completely within US borders. At nearly 1,000 feet at its deepest, the lake never freezes all the way across—a distance of about 30 miles at the southern end. To get a true sense of Lake Michigan, take a walk along the lakefront from Navy Pier to the Museum Campus. The lake's moods change daily, but it is always beautiful.

CENTRAL CHICAGO

Hotels
- 🏨 The Essex Inn
- 🏨 Sutton Place Hotel
- 🏨 Wheeler Mansion

Restaurants
- ❶ Ambria
- ❷ Cafe Ba-Ba-Reeba!
- ❸ Charlie Trotter's
- ❹ Chicago Pizza and Oven Grinder
- ❺ Ed Debevic's
- ❻ Gino's East
- ❼ Green Door Tavern
- ❽ Lou Mitchell's
- ❾ Mr. Beef
- ❿ Pluton
- ⓫ The Pump Room
- ⓬ The Third Coast
- ⓭ Topolobampo
- ⓮ Twin Anchors
- ⓯ Wishbone

Chicago Water Tower and Pumping Station★

On either side of N. Michigan Ave., at Chicago Ave.

In 1850s Chicago, contaminated water took its toll on human health and city development. In 1855 city sewage commissioners decided to bring in fresh lake water by building a tunnel extending two miles out under Lake Michigan. A huge water intake "crib" (50 feet by 70 feet) was built on land and floated out to be firmly grounded into the lake bottom at a depth of 40 feet. (From the shoreline, you can see the original crib's successors up and down the lakefront.) A tunnel was then built 6 feet under the lakebed to connect the crib with the pumping station and provide the city with fresh water from the lake. Ridiculed by naysayers, the plan came to be recognized as a masterpiece of engineering.

Now dwarfed by high rises, the castle-like structures of the Chicago Water Tower and Pumping Station (built in the late 1860s) were the only two public buildings to survive the 1871 fire. Today a lovely park surrounds the tower, while the pumping station, though still operational, has been refitted as the home of **Lookingglass Theatre** *(312-337-0665; www.lookingglasstheatre.org)* and a visitor information center *(163 E. Pearson St.; open year-round daily 7:30am–7pm; 312-742-8811).*

Chicago River Tours

One of the first things you'll notice as you walk around Chicago is the river that girdles the north and west sides of the Loop and divides it from the Magnificent Mile. Much cleaner than it once was, the Chicago River flows backwards from Lake Michigan (engineers reversed its flow in 1900 to keep waste out of the lake, which is the source of the city's drinking water). The river is now spanned by some 52 movable bridges, each one an engineering marvel.

Condos and restaurants line its banks, the pleasant **Riverwalk**★ winds along beside it, and great works of urban architecture loom above it. To enjoy these stunning vistas,

take an **Architecture River Cruise** with the Chicago Architecture Foundation. The lively 90-minute tours depart at least six times daily, rain or shine, from May 1 to the end of November from the dock located at the southeast corner of the Michigan Avenue Bridge and Wacker Drive *(reservations recommended: 312-902-1500; for details, contact the Architecture Foundation: 312-922-3432 or www.architecture.com).*

Wrigley Field★

1060 W. Addison St. 773-404-2827. www.chicago.cubs.com. For ticket information, see Musts for Fun.

Built as Weeghman Field in 1914 for the Chicago Whales of the Federal League before being occupied by the Cubs of the National League two years later, this stadium is an icon for baseball lovers everywhere. It's the oldest surviving National League ballpark and second only to Boston's Fenway Park (1912) overall. The Chicago Bears played football here from their beginnings in 1921 until 1970 before moving to Soldier Field in 1971. Famous for its ivy walls and lovable losing teams, the stadium is surrounded by turn-of-the-20C flats rather than the usual sea of parking lots. Many of the adjacent buildings boast rooftop clubs where ticket buyers watch the game over the outfield walls. The first night game was played here in 1988 after a long battle with neighbors to keep lights out of the field. Current talk revolves around moving Wrigley's walls out 10 feet— is nothing sacred?

Billy Goat's Curse

It all started when officials refused to admit restaurateur William Sianis and his billy goat, Murphy, into Game 4 of the World Series at Wrigley Field in 1945. "Cubs, they not gonna win anymore," declared Sianis, and the team lost the series (to the Detroit Tigers) and never returned. Though several attempts have been made to lift the curse by allowing descendants of Murphy into Wrigley, the whammy endures. As does the **Billy Goat Tavern** *(430 N. Michigan Ave., lower level; 312-222-1525)*, founded by "Billy Goat" Sianis in 1934. The haunt of reporters and night owls, and the inspiration for John Belushi's immortal "cheezborger, cheep, no Coke, Pepsi" routine on *Saturday Night Live*, the subterranean tavern (now run by Sianis' nephew, Sam) is also a favorite with tourists. No health food here, but a real, greasy slice of Chicago history. In the words of the late Chicago newspaper columnist Mike Royko, the late-night regulars at this tavern ". . . don't even drink cocktails, at least not in Billy Goat's, where the 'in' drink is still a shot and a beer."

Museums

Chicago takes justifiable pride in its array of museums; indeed, you could spend a week and not do them all justice. Some command majestic profiles on the lakefront; others grace parks and neighborhoods around the city. From earthly fossils to celestial bodies, Chicago's museums can indulge most any cultural pleasure.

Art Institute of Chicago★★★

111 S. Michigan Ave. 312-443-3600. www.artic.edu/aic. Open year-round Mon–Fri 10:30am–4:30pm (Thu until 8pm), Sat–Sun 10am–5pm. Closed Thanksgiving Day & Dec 25. $12 adults; $7 children (free for children ages 5 and under). Free admission Tue.

One of the great museums of the world and the preeminent arts institution of the Midwest, the Art Institute of Chicago (AIC) is a comprehensive center for arts education and exhibition. Its collections span 5,000 years and draw on the cultures of Europe, Asia, Africa and the Americas. If you're a lover of the Impressionist period, this is the place for you: the museum's reputation rests primarily on its collection of Impressionist and post-Impressionist paintings, one of the largest and most important outside France. Immerse yourself in a gallery or two, or sample a variety of the institute's visual delights.

Founded as one of the first art schools in the US in 1866 (the School of the Art Institute remains a world-class facility), the AIC was reorganized to include a museum in 1879. The grand World's Columbian Exposition of 1893 provided the perfect opportunity for trustees to construct the glorious temple of art that stands on Michigan Avenue today, guarded by the bronze lions cast by sculptor Edward Kemeys in 1894. From the 50,000 square feet of the original Allerton Building, the institute has expanded to encompass more than 400,000 square feet, spanning the block between Michigan Avenue and Columbus Drive. A new wing is slated to add another 60,000 square feet on the building's north side by 2007.

Eat Your Art Out

For a quick sandwich, grill selection, pizza or salad (and best for kids), visit the self-service **Café** on the lower level. The **Garden Restaurant** *(lower level; 312-553-9675)* features table service, a full bar, and a menu of contemporary American and seafood dishes. During the summer, the restaurant flings wide its doors onto the shady McKinlock Court for alfresco dining. Enter at Columbus Drive if you are only dining.

Heart of the Art Institute

Chinese, Japanese and Korean Collection★★★ — These galleries on the first floor cover nearly 5,000 years of artistic achievement on the opposite side of the world. A stunning collection of Chinese and Korean **ceramics**★ spans 1,800 years.

19C European Painting★★★ From Goya to Gauguin, these 12 second-floor galleries sparkle with painterly genius. Check out the breathtaking array of Impressionists in gallery 201, and the **Helen Birch Bartlett Memorial Collection**★★ of post-Impressionist and early 20C masterpieces in gallery 205.

American Arts★★ — Beginning with a delightful gallery of folk art, these exhibits chronicle the development of American taste through furniture, decorative arts, paintings and sculpture.

Contemporary and Modern Art★★ — These works, produced in Europe and America since 1900, are located in various halls around the museum. They provide a diverse survey of modern painting, sculpture and multimedia works, from the eerie landscapes of Dalí to the monumental canvases of Mark Rothko.

European Decorative Arts★★ — This collection is a trove of household, decorative and religious objects produced since 1100 AD. Check out the delectable **Rubloff Paperweight Collection**★, which looks good enough to eat.

European Painting and Sculpture★★ — Renaissance and Baroque masterpieces occupy the other half of the second floor. They trace the development of Western painting from flat medieval landscapes to the flamboyance of the Rococo. Don't miss works by Botticelli, Rembrandt and El Greco.

Touring Tip: Visiting the Art Institute

The museum's main entrance is on Michigan Avenue, across from Adams Street. Just inside you'll find an information desk with helpful docents and schedules of temporary exhibits, lectures and special events or tours. This is also the location of the ticket booth; the checkroom (be ready to check all purses, bags, umbrellas, baby carriers, backpacks and briefcases); and the main gift shop, well stocked with books, posters and a wide selection of beautifully crafted jewelry.

The collections are displayed in the Allerton Building and in three major additions, Gunsaulus Hall and the Rubloff and Rice buildings to the east. Buildings are connected only on the first floor. Just beyond the main entry foyer is the grand staircase, the point of departure for the general introduction tour. To explore the museum at your own pace, rent a Gallery Audio Guide *(at kiosks near both lobbies; $4)*, which will give you a comprehensive gallery overview.

Field Museum of Natural History★★★

1400 S. Lake Shore Dr. 312-922-9410. www.fieldmuseum.org. Open year-round daily 9am–5pm. Closed Dec 25. $19 adults, $9 children ages 4-11 (free for children 3 and under).

This world-class natural history institution occupies a suitably grand place at the south end of Grant Park. Known as the **Museum Campus★★★**, this area also includes the **Shedd Aquarium★★★** and the **Adler Planetarium★★**. Nine acres of exhibit halls and over 20 million artifacts await you in the temple-like building completed in 1921 by architect Daniel Burnham. Dinosaur bones, artifacts from cultures around the world and animal taxidermy have all been incorporated into fun, modern exhibits, though some galleries await updating. Even if only four percent of the collections are on exhibit when you go, there's still plenty to see!

A Dino Named Sue★★ – The museum's famous *Tyrannosaurus rex* skeleton occupies the place of honor on the main floor in Stanley Field Hall. You can't miss Sue—she's the one standing 13 feet tall at the hip with the menacing grin! For more on Sue and her ilk, visit the second-floor galleries just above her. There you'll be able to get a close look at her actual skull, which, weighing in at 600 pounds, is too heavy to display on the skeleton.

Touring Tip: Getting to the Museum Campus

You could easily spend a week here, but if you have the budget and the energy, you can sample all three museums in one day. By **car**, enter the campus at 18th Street from Lake Shore Drive. Follow signs to parking *($12 daily)*. Arrive by 9:30am and get discounted parking *($9)* at the Adler Lot and the North Garage. If you're early *and* lucky, you may find long-term metered parking *(25¢ for 30min)* along Solidarity Drive between the aquarium and the planetarium. Be warned: all parking bets are off during Chicago Bears home games at neighboring Soldier Field.

By **public transportation**, take the 146, 12, 127, 6 or 130 buses, or the CTA Red, Orange and Green Lines and the Metra Electric and South Shore commuter lines to Roosevelt Road; it's an easy walk from there. Daily throughout the summer, and over holidays and weekends year-round, **free trolleys** run to the campus from designated stops downtown. Or take a **water taxi** from Navy Pier *(all-day adult pass $12; children under 12, $3)*. Check out www.museumcampus.org for maps and details.

Outstanding in the Field

Africa★★ – This kaleidoscopic exhibit ventures from the streets of Dakar, Senegal, to the sand dunes of the Sahara. The sweeping presentation investigates African politics, art, environment, wildlife, commerce and family life by high-lighting the diverse cultures of the continent.

Eskimos and Northwest Coast Indians★★ – A seemingly endless display of masks, totem poles, articles of clothing and other Native American artifacts contrasts life in the Arctic and the Northwest.

Dino Zone★★ – At this new exhibit you can touch dinosaur bones and teeth, and test your knowledge of dino trivia. When the exhibit is complete in 2006, it will incorporate the newest scientific research about early life on Earth.

Hall of Gems★ – Everyone loves these shimmering precious and semiprecious stones, lusciously illuminated in a small darkened space.

Nature Walk★ – The specimens and dioramas at the Field are second to none; they take you on a trek through woods, wetlands and other wild places.

Plants of the World★ – This display will dazzle you with the incredible variety of form, color and function of the world's plants.

Traveling the Pacific★ and **Pacific Spirits**★ – These adjacent exhibits show-case the museum's collections from the cultures of the South Pacific. The highlight is the 1881 **Maori meeting house**, moved from New Zealand and recon-structed here piece by piece.

Underground Adventure★ – *Additional charge applies.* Walk among the creepy crawlies that live beneath our feet (simulated, of course) and get a bug's-eye view of life in the dirt.

Museum Campus Eats

You'll have plenty of choices for lunch during your Museum Campus visit. Enjoy fresh sandwiches (or take a coffee break) in the shadow of Sue the T-rex at the Field Museum's **Corner Bakery**. (If the kids vote for **McDonald's**, you'll find it in the base-ment.) Visit the **Bubble Net Food Court** at the Shedd Aquarium for pizza, burgers and the like. For the only table service on the Museum Campus, try **Soundings Restaurant** at the Shedd Aquarium. The menu features gourmet sandwiches, soups—and, yes, seafood—wine and cocktails in an attractive dining room overlooking the lake *(if you wish to dine but not visit the aquarium, reservations are required: 312-692-3277).* **Galileo Café** at the Adler Planetarium offers cafeteria-style sandwiches, salads and soups as well as a stunning view. Or bring your own picnic supplies and dine alfresco on the campus grounds in summer.

John G. Shedd Aquarium★★★

1200 S. Lake Shore Dr. 312-559-0200. www.shedd.org. Open Memorial Day–Labor Day daily 9am–6pm. Rest of the year daily 9am–5pm. Closed Dec 25. All-access pass: $23 adults, $17 children (ages 3-11). Admission is discounted for Chicago residents.

Hard by Lake Michigan, the Shedd Aquarium brings the ocean to the lakefront. As the world's largest indoor aquarium, it houses aquatic creatures from around the globe—from tiny, jewel-like spiny lobsters to 1,500-pound beluga whales. The Shedd's exhibits and programs emphasize conservation and the environment, and its remarkable animals bring the message vividly to life. The building opened in 1930 and resembles a monument to the Roman sea god, Neptune, whose trident tops the roof. Inside, keep an eye out for decorative wave and shell patterns and charming sea creatures that crawl over light fixtures, tiles and doorways. A pioneer at re-creating aquatic habitats, the Shedd has transformed many of its older exhibits into mini-ecosystems that support not only fish but plants, birds and a furry surprise or two.

Touring Tip

Arrive early when you visit this popular attraction; it gets especially crowded during the summer and on weekends. Plan your visit for Sunday morning if you really want to avoid the lines.

To save a few bucks, go for the Shedd's **Discount Days** on Monday and Tuesday from mid-September to the end of February. On these days, general admission is free and admission to the Oceanarium and Wild Reef exhibits is offered at a discount *($15 adults, $10 children)*.

No Silly Animal Tricks

Shedd animal behaviorists are adamant about the motive behind the Marine Mammal Presentations in the Oceanarium. The behaviors you'll see are not "tricks"; they reflect natural activities of the animals, including diving, spyhopping and tailwalking. The narration explains how these behaviors relate to marine mammal survival in the wild (a spyhopping dolphin, for instance, stands straight up on its tail for a better view above the water). The animals are also taught certain behaviors to make medical exams easier on them and on the keepers. *Oceanarium shows are held Mon–Fri 10:30am, 12pm, 1:30pm & 3:30pm; weekends 10:30am, 12pm, 1:30pm, 3pm & 4:30pm.*

Dive In!

When you buy your admission ticket, you'll receive a schedule of feedings, demonstrations and shows for that day.

Oceanarium★★ – This amazing habitat re-creates a Pacific Northwest ecosystem. Stroll "along the coast," following the edge of the oversized pools where beluga whales, Pacific white-sided dolphins and harbor seals carouse. The wide expanse of Lake Michigan stretches beyond, a vista barely interrupted by the oceanarium's glass wall. Beneath the pools, underwater-viewing galleries bring you nose to snout with graceful dolphins. And be prepared to laugh at the penguin habitat, where beguiling rockhoppers, magellenics and gentoos go about their business, diving, swimming and waddling.

Wild Reef★★ – The newest of Shedd's world ecosystems, this extraordinary exhibit takes you deep into a Philippine coral reef to see one of the world's most diverse habitats. Displays explain the life cycle of the reef and illustrate how living corals form, survive and die. A huge wall of water teeming with gemlike fish against a backdrop of artificial coral bends around the space. See sharks up close and personal in the impressive tank around the corner, and watch underfoot to see little stingrays darting and gliding. So as not to harvest coral from the wild, the Shedd grows (or fabricates) its own.

Amazon Rising: Seasons of the River★ – In these galleries you'll experience a year in the life of an Amazon floodplain forest. Habitats are stocked with some 250 species, including a huge anaconda and a tiny pigmy marmoset.

Caribbean Reef★ – If you stare long enough into these 90,000 gallons of fishy fun, you might spot all of the 500 tropical fish that live there, including hammerhead sharks, rays, and a sea turtle named Nickel *(see sidebar, below)*. Stick around for feeding time, which happens five times a day.

Best of the Beasts

Of course you won't want to miss the dolphins, whales and sharks, but don't overlook some of the less obvious aquatic wonders at the Shedd. Our favorites include **Nickel** the Lucky Sea Turtle, who lives in the Caribbean Reef tank. You'll know her by her "limp," a reminder of injuries from which she is recovering. The name? During her rehab, vets found a nickel lodged in her throat. And be sure to pay your respects to Granddad, the 80-year-old lungfish who arrived at the aquarium as a youngster in 1933. Oh, and those green things you see in many habitats? They're heads of romaine lettuce—a favorite treat among certain residents.

Museum of Science and Industry★★★

57th St., at S. Lake Shore Dr. 773-684-1414. www.msichicago.org. Open year-round Memorial Day–Labor Day Mon–Sat 9:30am–5:30pm, Sun 11am–5:30pm. Rest of the year Mon–Sat 9:30am–4pm, Sun 11am–4pm. Closed Dec 25. $9 adults, $5 children (ages 3-11). Free admission Mon. Additional charge for Omnimax Theater & special exhibits.

This noisy hall of wonders and widgets is one of Chicago's most popular attractions, and the crowds prove it. Since 1933, the "MSI" has occupied the only building left standing after the World's Columbian Exposition of 1893 *(see p 58)*. Designed in the grand classical style by Charles B. Atwood as the Palace of Fine Arts, the building fell into disrepair until 1926 when the idea to house an "industrial" museum there took root. Over the years the museum has collected an amazing array of oddities and artifacts—from a miniature **Fairy Castle**★ to the world's fastest car. Today, spread out over four floors, the MSI covers topics in transportation, the human body, technology and manufacturing, communication, energy and environment, and space and defense. *For a description of exhibits, see Musts for Kids.*

Touring Tip: Visiting MSI

This can be an intimidating museum to navigate efficiently because of its size and layout. Pick up a floor plan and purchase entry, special-exhibit and **Omnimax** tickets as you enter the Great Hall from the underground garage. Plan to see the **Coal Mine**★★, **Idea Factory** and **U-505 Submarine**★—all timed-entry exhibits—early, since lines for these can develop fast. In the Great Hall, you can check your coat, rent a stroller, and visit the gift shop before you ascend the escalator, elevators or stairs to the ground level. Exhibits, restrooms and cafeteria-style dining can be found on this floor. From here, the museum complex takes in the **Henry Crown Space Center** and three floors within the central, east and west pavilions. The floors are connected by four color-coded stairwells off the rotunda of the central pavilion (the elevator is in the red stairwell). East of the central pavilion, the Crown Center connects to the pavilions by a hallway accessible from the ground floor.

Adler Planetarium★★

1300 S. Lake shore Dr. 312-922-7827. www.adlerplanetarium.org. Open year-round Mon–Fri 9:30am–4:30pm, weekends 9am–4:30pm. Closed Thanksgiving Day & Dec 25. $18 adults, $16 children (ages 4-17); fee includes admission and two sky shows.

It's worth the **views**★★ up and down the lakefront to walk out to the Adler, which occupies a beautiful setting. The oldest planetarium in the Western Hemisphere, it is also renowned for its fine collection of historic astronomical instruments and its splendid sky shows.

Chicago's planetarium sprang from philanthropist Max Adler's belief that a Zeiss projector (used for re-creating the night sky on an enclosed dome) would be a wonderful teaching tool for the city. He donated $1 million, and architect Ernest A. Grunsfeld Jr. designed a compact, red-granite jewel for the dramatic setting at the tip of Northerly Island. A major renovation in 1999 added 60,000 square feet of wraparound exhibit space that enclosed two-thirds of the old Art Deco building in glass. As you make your way through the new space, notice the charming bronze signs of the zodiac that still adorn each corner of the original 12-sided structure.

The Sky's the Limit

StarRider® Theater★★ – Located on the lower level, "the world's first inter-active computer-graphics theater" immerses you in the stars on its domed screen. Here you'll voyage through the universe, land on Mars or visit the tombs and temples of ancient Egypt.

History of Astronomy Gallery★ – *Lower level.* This gallery showcases the planetarium's extensive collection of curious historic instruments for measuring time, earth and space. If more modern space exploration suits your taste, visit **CyberSpace**, where news about the latest Mars landings and space-probe discoveries are broadcast at VisionStations.

Touring Tip

You'll want to leave some time to explore the rest of the museum as well, which can be a challenge to figure out because of the shape of the space (be sure to pick up a floor plan at the admissions desk). On the upper level, interactive exhibits attempt to demystify the universe, the Milky Way galaxy and our solar system. Lower-level exhibits journey through the history of Western astronomy as well as the importance of sky study to ancient cultures.

Museums

Oriental Institute★★

1155 E. 58th St., at University Ave., on the University of Chicago campus. 773-702-9514. www.oi.uchicago.edu. Open year-round Tue–Sat 10am–6pm, Sun noon–6pm. Closed Mon & major holidays.

While the institute is dedicated to the study of languages, history and cultures of the ancient Near East, its museum contains one of the world's choicest collections of Near Eastern art and antiquities. Most of its 75,000 artifacts were collected by institute archaeologists, including James Henry Breasted, who led the University of Chicago's first field expedition to the land we now know as Iraq in 1904 and created the institute in 1919. The institute has resided in its current building on the University of Chicago campus since 1931. The museum galleries have been undergoing extensive renovation over the past few years; so far only the **Egyptian, Mesopotamian** and **Persian** exhibits have reopened.

David and Alfred Smart Museum of Art★

5550 S. Greenwood Ave., on the University of Chicago campus. 773-702-0200. www.smartmuseum.uchicago.edu. Open mid-Jun–mid-Sept Tue–Fri 10am–4pm, weekends 11am–5pm. Rest of the year Tue, Wed & Fri 10am–4pm, Thu 10am–8pm, weekends 11am–5pm. Closed Mon.

Opened in 1974 and named for the founders of *Esquire* magazine, this small jewel of a university museum holds 7,500 pieces spanning 5,000 years. The Smart Museum rotates its permanent collection, which excels in arts of the late 19C and early 20C, among its four major galleries.

University of Chicago★★

From 55th St. on the north to 60th St. on the south, between Dorchester & Maryland Aves. The main quad lies along 58th St., between Ellis & University Aves.

This handsome 190-acre urban campus is steeped in history, reputation and, well, Nobel Prizes (78 have been awarded to students, researchers and faculty—more than any other school). Founded in 1890 with a strong academic vision, the U of C blossomed early into one of the nation's leading research schools. In the early 1940s, the abandoned football grandstands concealed the Manhattan Project laboratory of Enrico Fermi, whose team of physicists achieved the first self-sustaining nuclear reaction. Immerse yourself in collegiate atmosphere with lunch at **Medici** *(1327 E. 57th St.; 773-667-7394)*, where students have gathered to eat pizza and burgers for decades.

48 MICHELIN MUST SEES

Chicago Historical Society★

1601 N. Clark St., at North Ave. 312-642-4600. www.chicagohs.org. Open year-round Mon–Sat 9:30am–4:30pm, Sun noon–5pm. Closed Jan 1, Thanksgiving Day & Dec 25. $5.

Want to delve deeper into Chicago's past? Then don't miss a visit to the Chicago Historical Society, located at the southwestern corner of Lincoln Park. Organized in 1856, the city's oldest cultural institution covers America until 1865 and Chicago since the first explorers. Its collections are chock-full of documents and objects connected to Chicago's first settlers, as well as historic photographs, memorabilia from Chicago's two world's fairs, and, of course, the Chicago Fire. A major renovation is planned for the historical society's permanent **Chicago and American History galleries** on the second floor, which will close all or portions of them to the public in 2005.

> **Lunch at Big Shoulders**
>
> *312-587-7766.* Light and healthy lunches (including children's specials) compete with great views of Lincoln Park in this cafe, set in a two-story glass-enclosed turret at the Chicago Historical Society. Notice the re-creation of the massive archway framing the inside doorway; it once marked the entrance to the Union Stockyards, site of Chicago's infamous slaughterhouses in the 19C.

Museum of Contemporary Art★

220 E. Chicago Ave. 312-280-2660. www.mcachicago.org. Open year-round Wed–Sun 10am–5pm (Tue until 8pm). Closed Mon, Jan 1, Thanksgiving Day & Dec 25. $10 .

The task of presenting the avant-garde can be daunting, but the MCA does a good job of making the works and movements of the art of our time accessible to everyone through thoughtful label writing, audio programming and free guided tours *(check schedule at desk)*. Exhibits mounted on a rotating basis from the museum's 7,000-piece permanent collection generally occupy the third- and fourth-floor galleries. Much of what you'll see focuses on new acquisitions and works by living artists, but the museum's collection also includes the art of Marcel Duchamp, Max Ernst, René Magritte, Alexander Calder, Andy Warhol and a host of Chicago and Illinois artists such as Ed Paschke, June Leaf and Jim Nutt.

> **Puck's**
>
> *On the east side of the Museum of Contemporary Art.* Overlooking the sculpture garden and Lake Michigan beyond through an expansive glass wall, Puck's features fine dining with a view. The menu highlights Wolfgang Puck's signature Chinois chicken salad and a selection of specialty pizzas along with salads and sandwiches *(reservations recommended; 312-397-4034; www.mcachicago.org).*

Peggy Notebaert Nature Museum★

2430 N. Cannon Dr. 773-755-5100. www.naturemuseum.org. Open year-round Mon–Fri 9am–4:30pm, weekends 10am–5pm. Closed Jan 1, Thanksgiving Day & Dec 25. $7 adults, $4 children (ages 3-12). Free admission Thu.

Beautifully sited on Lincoln Park, along the lower end of North Pond, this sand-colored "cluster of wedge-shaped blocks" was designed to resemble the sand dunes that once covered this area. Opened in 1999, the museum aims to help visitors "think green" through environmental learning and an appreciation of our dwindling natural resources. Inside, six permanent exhibits fill two levels; outside, pathways wind through native plantings.

Butterfly Haven★ – The air on the second floor is aflutter with 70 species of butterflies, many so beautiful you may mistake them for flowers. Watch out: one of the residents might just hitch a ride on your shoulder! Check out the chrysalis case and talk to the interpreter. If a chrysalis is hatching while you're visiting, you'll be spellbound by the process.

Wilderness Walk – Ants and other live bugs and creatures, along with walk-through dioramas, help you to picture the sand dunes, prairies and savannas native to the greater Chicago area.

RiverWorks – To get the lowdown on the Chicago River and other similar waterways, visit this first-floor exhibit, where you—and the kids—can splash around and create dams, locks, run-offs and, yes, even sewers.

Dining with the Prairie School

Tucked away in Lincoln Park just a short way north of the nature museum sits a romantic little restaurant called **North Pond** *(2610 N. Cannon Dr.; 773-477-5845; www.northpondrestaurant.com)*. Once a skaters' warming hut on the edge of—you guessed it—North Pond, the building still serves as a cozy retreat from winter's chill, as well as a cool oasis in summer. Beautifully renovated in Prairie style with warm oak, copper and art-glass accents, the space now houses an elegant eatery that features local and regional ingredients and wines from small American vineyards. Tall windows look out over the pond, the park and the city skyline, and a fieldstone fireplace completes the ambience. Be sure to reserve a table in the front room if you wish to dine with the best view and near a roaring fire in winter.

Smith Museum of Stained-Glass Windows★

On Navy Pier, 600 E. Grand Ave. at Lake Michigan. 312-595-5024. Open year-round Mon–Thu 10am–8pm, Fri & Sat 10am–10pm, Sun 10am–7pm.

In the market for windows? Filling a series of galleries along the lower-level terraces of Festival Hall, this unique museum showcases more than 100 stained-glass windows from 1897 to the present, all works of art in themselves. Their creators include well-known names such as Louis Comfort Tiffany and John LaFarge, as well as Chicago artists Ed Paschke and Roger Brown.

DuSable Museum of African American History

740 E. 56th Pl. 773-947-0600. www.dusablemuseum.org. Open year-round Mon–Sat 10am–5pm, Sun noon–5pm. Closed Jan 1, Thanksgiving Day & Dec 25. $3. Free admission Sun.

Founded in 1961 by Dr. Margaret Goss Burroughs in her home, this cultural and historical museum now occupies a former park administration building. The modern Harold Washington Wing, added to the structure's south side in 1992, houses cultural programs that supplement permanent and traveling exhibits on African-American life, art and history.

Mexican Fine Arts Center Museum

1852 W. 19th St. 312-738-1503. www.mfacmchicago.org. Open year-round Tue, Thu–Sun 10am–5pm, Wed 10am–8pm. Closed Mon & major holidays.

The largest institution of its kind in the US, this respected ethnic center is best known for its exhibits and programs focusing on Mexico's colorful celebration of the Day of the Dead *(see sidebar below)*. A recent 33,000-square-foot addition enables the museum to exhibit works from its permanent collection in **Mexicanidad: Our Past Is Present**, which journeys from prehistory to the present. Note the stunning beaded mural called *New Awakening*.

Dia de los Muertos

Day of the Dead (celebrated from October 31 to November 2) is a time of great festivity in Mexico, and it's a lot of fun at the Mexican Fine Arts Center, too. A blend of ancient Aztec and Christian rituals, including feasting, parades, and the building of colorful home altars, the holiday honors the spirits of those who have died. Women bake skeleton-shaped bread, and children crave *calaveras*, grinning candy skulls. Families visit and decorate cemeteries, singing and dancing as a way of scorning death. The museum celebrates the season annually with demonstrations, programs and an exhibition of Day of the Dead crafts—incorporating symbols such as skulls, skeletons and marigolds.

Urbs in Horto, City in a Garden, has long been Chicago's nickname, and you'll see why when you experience the city's parks and gardens—old, new and renewed. Park District gardeners plant over 550,000 annuals and perennials and 156,000 bulbs each year, along with 8,000 trees and shrubs. As a result, sweeping greens spaces, pocket parks, and even the medians and parkways of major thoroughfares such as Lake Shore Drive blossom with color.

Millennium Park★★★

Bounded by Michigan Ave., Randolph & Monroe Sts. and Columbus Dr. Open year-round daily 6am–11pm. 312-742-1168. www.millenniumpark.org.

Mayor Richard J. Daley's "park du triomphe" opened in the summer of 2004 to boisterous acclaim from critics and public alike. In spite of some grumbling about the gargantuan ($475 million!) price tag, most everyone agrees that the park is indeed a triumph. By day or night (it's beautifully illuminated in the evenings), this is no ordinary park. Though not one for pets (dogs are forbidden), the park's 24.5 acres beckon at every turn with something to see, touch or experience. Crowded with delights, Millennium Park offers an escape from the daily grind. And it serves another more practical purpose by masking an unsightly area of railroad tracks and parking lots that now operate below the park's well-manicured surface.

Best of the Millennium

Jay Pritzker Pavilion★★★ – Above all, literally, hovers the metallic mayhem of architect Frank Gehry's proscenium arch that marks this state-of-the-art outdoor theater. Sails, clouds, a cherry bomb in a soda can—everyone has an opinion about Gehry's oversized scramble of stainless steel, and you will too. The theater accommodates 4,000 in fixed seats and 7,000 on the oval-shaped fairway, which is covered with a trellis that holds speakers up and out of the way. This "waterproof" lawn is specially designed to drain away rainwater in 15 minutes. Gehry's 120-foot overhanging "headdress" shelters the stage itself, which is lined with pine wood. It's even air conditioned for the comfort of the **Grant Park Orchestra and Chorus** *(312-742-7638; www.grantparkmusicfesitval.com)*, which holds free concerts at the Pavilion throughout the summer.

Cloud Gate★★★ – Affectionately known as the Bean, this sculpture by Anish Kapoor has become the surprise favorite of the park. The gleaming structure of stainless steel —66 feet long, 33 feet high and weighing 110 tons—draws visitors like moths to a flame. Its jelly-bean shape creates fantastic reflections of the city skyline and the crowds—go ahead, walk up and

pick yourself out. Better yet, step under the Bean and gaze up into its shiny underbelly. The effect is a kind of cross between a city gate, a majestic rotunda ceiling and a carnival mirror.

BP Bridge★★ – Getting there is all the fun on this meandering bridge designed by Frank Gehry. In 925 feet of luxurious serpentine curves, the bridge connects Millennium and Grant parks over Columbus Drive. It's clad in stainless-steel panels that enclose walkers without the need for handrails. The broad hardwood deck slopes gently, inviting you to pause and take in the cityscape from every angle. Kids love to run the length of it (though this is frowned upon). The bridge also buffers the Pritzker Pavilion from traffic noise.

Crown Fountain★★ – And for something completely different, check out the Crown Fountain, where huge projected faces spit water out of their mouths like modern gargoyles. The two 50-foot towers of steel, glass, light and water are the work of Spanish artist Jaume Plensa, and don't sound nearly as pleasing as they are in person. Best of all, a shallow, black-granite reflecting pool between the towers proves wonderful for wading and splashing as kids quickly discover. Watch carefully as the faces (a total of 300, soon to be 1,000), all Chicagoans, change slowly over the course of several minutes.

Lurie Garden★ – This planted sanctuary is truly a work in progress since the perennials will take a year or two to fill in and the protective pine hedgerow, known as the Shoulder Hedge, requires about 10 years to mature. From the hedge, the garden slopes gently to the south to maximize its sun. A wooden boardwalk and watery pools, called the Seam, bisect the planted spaces.

Grant Park★★

Bounded by Roosevelt Rd. & Randolph St. on the north and south, and Michigan Ave. & Lake Shore Dr. on the west. 312-742-7650. www.chicagoparkdistrict.com.

Overshadowed now by its glitzy neighbor Millennium Park, Grant Park remains nonetheless dignified and beautiful in an old-fashioned sort of way. The city's 319-acre "front yard" marks roughly the midpoint in the swath of parks that trims Chicago's 28-mile lakeshore. The park has been shaped by landfill, accretion, erosion and the human hand since 1830 when state commissioners set aside a thin strip of land along the shoreline to "remain forever open, clear and free." Sixty years later, mail-order magnate A. Montgomery Ward conducted a lengthy and successful battle with the city to clear the stables, railroad tracks and other eyesores that had rooted there in spite of the old edict.

In 1909 architect Daniel Burnham drew up a comprehensive plan for the city of Chicago calling for a "formal focal point," and the elegant landscaping of the park began to emerge as construction started in 1915. Though the automobile age sliced up the green space with busy streets, the park still offers peaceful gardens, picnic spots and lovely vistas of the city and lake. Tennis courts and a playground occupy the park's shady northeast corner.

Fests, Feasts and Fun in Grant Park

Throughout the summer months, Grant Park is *the* place to be for Chicagoans and visitors. Topping the list of special events is **Taste of Chicago**, which attracts more than 3 million people over 10 days to sample local eats (skip this festival on July 3 and 4 unless you enjoy a mob). No admission fee is charged, and food vendors take only tickets, so if you wish to taste, purchase tickets with cash or credit at any of several booths.

Grant Park also hosts Chicago's renowned music festivals, all held at the **Petrillo Bandshell** and featuring headline entertainment free of charge:

Chicago Blues Festival, 1st weekend in June

Chicago Gospel Festival, June

Chicago Country Music Festival, during the Taste of Chicago (late June into early July)

Chicago Jazz Festival, Labor Day Weekend

What's What in Grant Park

Museum Campus★★★ – The southern part of the park is home to the city's popular triad of museums: **Field Museum of Natural History**★★★, **Shedd Aquarium**★★★, and **Adler Planetarium**★★ *(see Museums).*

Buckingham Fountain★★–
Columbus Dr. at Congress Pkwy.
Centerpiece of Grant Park, the Clarence Buckingham Memorial Fountain is truly a lakefront jewel. Donated to the city by philanthropist Kate Sturges Buckingham to honor her brother, the fountain was completed in 1927 at a cost of $750,000. A $2.8-million restoration completed in April 1995 returned the fountain to its original splendor. It's modeled on a fountain at the Palace of Versailles in France, but is nearly twice as large. Intended to represent Lake Michigan, the fountain pumps 1.5 million gallons from the lake, recirculating all but what's lost through spray and evaporation—stand downwind on a hot, windy day for a refreshing spritz. Three basins of Georgia pink marble rise from the main pool; gargantuan carvings of seaweed and shells encircle the out-

side of each basin. In the large pool, four bronze sea horses, each 20 feet long, represent the states that border the lake.

Water and Light

As spectacular as the fountain's monumental scale are the water-and-light shows that flow from the basin during the summer. The fountain's 134 jets pump water at a rate of 14,100 gallons a minute and the central jet shoots water skyward to create a dazzling effect *(May–Oct dusk–11pm; 312-747-2474)*. Once controlled entirely by hand, the choreography of water and light is now regulated by computer.

A Fountain of Facts

- Buckingham Fountain is among the largest fountains in the world.
- At its maximum, the center jet shoots up 150 feet.
- The bottom pool measures 280 feet across, the lower basin is 103 feet, the middle basin is 60 feet and the upper basin is 24 feet.
- In all, 820 lights color the fountain's water and light display.

Lincoln Park★★

Visitor Center is located at Lincoln Park Cultural Center, 2045 N. Lincoln Park West. 312-742-7726. www.chicagopark district.com. Open year-round Mon–Fri 9am–9pm, Sat 8am–4pm, Sun 10am–3pm.

Except for the occasional stray bone, it's hard to tell that this was once a soggy cemetery. Today the sweeping expanse is one of Chicago's most compelling landscapes. Unlike so many urban areas with waterfronts blighted by industry, Chicago provides unlimited access to the lake via its numerous lakefront parks. Among the finest is Lincoln Park.

The cemetery was established here in 1837, but as the city limits bulged northward from downtown, the cemetery's new neighbors lobbied for replacing it with parkland. Moving the corpses took time, but by the 1880s the heart of the park was well established. Filling in the land over the next decades extended the park to its northern limits by 1957. Today stretching 6 miles and 1,200 acres along the shoreline of Lake Michigan, from Oak Street north to Ardmore Avenue, Lincoln Park trims the city's watery edge with a pleasant and peaceful greenbelt. At North Avenue, the park forms the northern edge of the affluent **Gold Coast★** *(see Neighborhoods),* and at Clark Street, the eastern boundary of the lively **Lincoln Park/DePaul★** neighborhood, where theaters, restaurants and shops abound.

Café Brauer

2021 N. Stockton Dr. Open year-round daily 11am–5pm. 312-742-2480.

This cafe makes a good stopping point on your walk through the park for a fresh brew or a bite to eat. In summer you can enjoy the beer garden overlooking South Pond. Architect Dwight Perkins, whose other credits include some of the animal houses at Lincoln Park Zoo, designed this refectory in 1908 for restaurateurs Paul and Caspar Brauer. A striking example of the Prairie school style, it hugs the pond with its main pavilion and flanking loggias. Arts and Crafts details—chandeliers, tiles, mosaics and windows—lend the interior a suitably rustic charm.

Touring Tip

To enjoy much of what Lincoln Park has to offer, start at the **Standing Lincoln** between LaSalle Street and North Avenue and wend your way north to Diversey Parkway.

A Walk in the Park

Lincoln Park Zoo★★ – *2200 N. Cannon Dr. See Musts for Kids.*

Peggy Notebaert Nature Museum★ – *2430 N. Cannon Dr. See Museums.*

Alfred Caldwell Lily Pool★ – *Enter from the north off Fullerton Pkwy.* Step into this secret garden and enter another world. Originally planned in the Victorian style in the 1880s, the garden was reshaped as a wooded grove in 1937 by landscape architect Alfred Caldwell. The plot spent much of its life as the zoo's Rookery until Caldwell's Prairie-style vision was restored in 2002. Today this tranquil enclave is a haven for birds and bird-watchers alike.

Lincoln Park Conservatory – *2391 N. Stockton Dr. 312-742-7736. Open year-round daily 9am–5pm.* Modeled in 1892 on London's Crystal Palace, the glass and copper structure and its 15 propagating houses, greenhouses and gardens now cover three acres.

Garfield Park Conservatory★

300 N. Central Park Ave., in Garfield Park. 312-746-5100. www.garfield-conservatory.org. Open year-round daily 9am–5pm.

Built in 1908 by celebrated landscape architect Jens Jensen, Garfield Park Conservatory has become popular for exhibits that integrate sculpture or objects (such as dinosaur skeletons) into the foliage. Be sure to look for the work that renowned glass artist **Dale Chihuly** left behind in the Aroid House after his big show here in 2001. The conservatory mounts several shows a year, as well as market days on summer weekends.

Restoration of the conservatory has been underway for a while now, and the results are stunning; the newly renovated **Palm House**, for example, contains 3,500 plants.

All That Glitters

Wondering what that glittery gold structure located south of the conservatory beyond the elevated tracks is? Known as the "Gold Dome Building" *(100 N. Central Park Ave.)* for obvious reasons, it was built in 1928 as the headquarters of the West Park Commission. The structure serves today as the park's fieldhouse. Its sparkling gold dome now looks out of place in the gritty neighborhood that surrounds the park, but in its heyday the building was no doubt an elegant addition to the banks of the park's original lagoon.

Jackson Park

*E. 56th to 57th Sts., Stony Island Ave. to Lake Michigan.
www.chicagoparkdistrict.com.*

Located 8 miles south of the Loop along Lake Michigan's shoreline, the park's 600 acres of playing fields, lagoons and lush vegetation began as a wasteland of sand dunes and scrub marshes. Famed landscape architect Frederick Law Olmsted (designer of Central Park in New York City) first laid out the park in 1870. He later redesigned and completed it for the World's Columbian Exposition in 1893 *(see sidebar below)*, creating a series of lagoons and formal ponds as its centerpiece. In addition to the features that remain from the fair, Jackson Park now features a lovely 18-hole golf course *(see Musts for Outdoor Fun)*.

Fragments of the fair include **Columbia Basin**★, a reflecting pool designed by Olmsted for the Palace of Fine Arts, now the **Museum of Science and Industry**★★★ *(see Musts for Kids)*; **Osaka Gardens**★, at the north end of the sanctuary on Wooded Island; and **The Republic**★, the 24-foot-high "Golden Lady" cast by Daniel Chester French—the only sculpture in the park.

World's Columbian Exposition

In a spirited battle to host the 1893 World's Columbian Exposition, Chicago earned its enduring nickname "Windy City" because of all the blustery boasting that led to its winning the honor over New York, Washington and St. Louis. Conceived to celebrate the 400th anniversary of Columbus' discovery of America, this world's fair covered over 650 acres along present-day Jackson Park and encompassed some 200 buildings erected by leading architects. From its opening day on May 1, 1893, to its close in October, the exposition awed some 27 million visitors with its architecture and attractions, including the world's first Ferris wheel and the infamous "Little Egypt" dancing the hootchie kootchie. At night, floodlights illuminated the Neoclassical buildings, creating a sparkling white, fairylike atmosphere. But the fair was fleeting as its construction was done entirely of "staff," a temporary material left to crumble away at the event's end.

GREATER CHICAGO

GLENCOE, LAKE FOREST · Chicago Botanic Garden★★

WILMETTE

Baha'i House of Worship★★

★★NORTH SHORE

Northwestern University

EVANSTON

Rogers Park

LAKE

Lifeline Theatre

Devon Ave.

MICHIGAN

Rosehill Cemetery

UPTOWN · Wilson Skatepark
Graceland Cemetery★★
Lincoln Park★★

Puppet Parlor

★Wrigley Field

★LINCOLN PARK/ DEPAUL

Bailiwick Rep. Theater
Athenaeum Theatre

Apollo Theater

★Peggy Notebaert Nature Museum

MAGNIFICENT MILE ★★★

Vittum Theater

★Garfield Park Conservatory

United Center

THE LOOP ★★★

★★★OAK PARK

NEAR WEST SIDE

Mexican Fine Arts Center Museum ■

CHINATOWN

PILSEN

BRIDGEPORT CANARYVILLE

Burnham Skatepark
Burnham Park

U.S. Cellular Field

BRONZEVILLE

NEAR SOUTH SIDE

MIDWAY AIRPORT

HYDE PARK KENWOOD

Washington Park

★David and Alfred Smart Museum of Art

★★Robie House

★★★MUSEUM OF SCIENCE AND INDUSTRY

DuSable Museum of African-American History ■

★★UNIVERSITY OF CHICAGO

Jackson Park

Oriental Institute★★

Oak Woods Cemetery

EVERGREEN PARK

ILLINOIS
INDIANA

★PULLMAN HISTORIC DISTRICT

O'HARE AIRPORT

★★ Brookfield Zoo | Morton Arboretum ★

★ Illinois & Michigan Canal NHS

Hotels
1 City Suites Hotel
2 Hawthorne Terrace
3 The Homestead
4 Hotel Orrington
5 Majestic Hotel
6 The Willows Hotel
7 Wooded Isle Suites

Restaurants
1 Andies
2 Ann Sather
3 Aruns
4 Club Lucky
5 Davis Street Fishmarket
6 Erwin
7 Green Zebra
8 Half Shell
9 Healthy Food
10 Heaven on Seven
11 Hema's Kitchen
12 Pasteur
13 Tapas Barcelona
● Trio Atelier

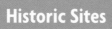
Chicago's fascinating history takes in industry and robber barons, immigrants and labor movements, and, of course, architecture. Here are some of our favorite sites from the city's past.

Graceland Cemetery★★

4001 N. Clark St., Lakeview. From downtown, take Lake Shore Dr. north and turn left on Irving Park Rd. to the cemetery. 773-525-1105. www.gracelandcemetery.org. Open year-round daily 8am–4:30pm. Closed Dec 25, July 4 & Labor Day.

For a slice of Chicago history, check out this cemetery, just north of Wrigley Field, where notable architecture and sculpture mark the resting places of many of the city's movers and shakers. Developed in 1860, Graceland received many of the corpses that were exhumed from the lakeshore cemetery where construction of Lincoln Park was underway. Stroll the 119-acre grounds yourself (pick up a site plan at the entrance) or check with the Chicago Architecture Foundation *(see p 32)* about its next Graceland tour. And no, Elvis is not buried here.

Notable Residents

Be sure to pay a visit to the tombs of Henry Harrison Getty and Martin Ryerson (both designed by Louis Sullivan), Marshall Field (designed by Daniel Chester French), Potter and Bertha Palmer, Daniel Burnham, Peter Schoenhofen and George Pullman *(see p 64)*, all in the northern half of the cemetery. To the south rest boxing great Jack Johnson and National League founder William Hulbert, who is spending eternity under a large baseball.

More Local Haunts

If Graceland shelters the mortal remains of Chicago's historic elite, the equally lovely **Rosehill** *(5800 N. Ravenswood Ave.; 773-561-5940)* hosts a cadre of local merchants, bankers and businessmen who made this the City that Works, including Oscar Mayer, Aaron Montgomery Ward and Richard Warren Sears. Many of Chicago's mayors rest here, along with Civil War generals and soldiers. Founded in 1859, Rosehill is Chicago's largest cemetery, covering 350 wooded acres. If the Gothic castle-like entryway looks familiar, it's because it replicates the **Water Tower and Pumping Station**★ downtown *(see Landmarks).*

On the city's South Side, **Oak Woods Cemetery** *(1035 E. 67th St.; 773-288-3800)* is even older (1854), and lodges some of the city's most interesting residents: Mayor Harold Washington, Chicago's first African-American mayor; crime boss Big Jim Colosimo; Olympian Jesse Owens; activist Ida B. Wells; and physicist Enrico Fermi. *For more about local cemeteries, visit www.graveyards.com.*

Robie House★★

5757 S. Woodlawn Ave., on the University of Chicago campus. Take Lake Shore Dr. south to 53rd St. and turn left on Woodlawn Ave. 708-848-1976. www.wrightplus.org. Visit by 1-hour guided tour only, year-round Mon–Fri 11am, 1pm & 3pm, weekends every 20min 11am–3:30pm. Closed Jan 1, Thanksgiving Day & Dec 25. $9. By bus, take #6 Jackson Park Express to Stony Island Ave. & 57th St.; walk west 6 blocks to Woodlawn Ave. and go left 1 block.

This home made its designer, **Frank Lloyd Wright**, world famous and helped "break the box" of traditional architecture. In 1908 wealthy inventor Frederick Robie commissioned architect Wright to design his residence in Hyde Park. The resulting home, with its distinctive horizontal lines, is considered a masterpiece of modern architecture.

The Robies lived here only for a year or so, after which time the house passed through a number of different owners. It was saved from the wrecking ball at the 11th hour in 1957 and is now operated by the University of Chicago in conjunction with the Frank Lloyd Wright Home and Studio Foundation, which is supervising an intensive 10-year restoration.

Inside, the hallmarks of the Prairie style are all here: the long, low horizontal lines, side-hinging casement windows, the hidden front entrance, built-in furniture and the grand hearth that separates living from dining space. Stained, leaded and art-glass windows are done in geometric patterns, and Wright's trademark globe-shaped "moonlight" ceiling fixtures provide lighting. Note the long Roman bricks that Wright favored, which accentuate the horizontal even more.

Can't Get Enough Frank Lloyd Wright?

Calling all FLW fans. You've been to Robie House. You've been to Oak Park *(see Excursions)*. But wait, there's more. A handful of Wright's residential architecture (all privately owned) still stands in Chicago, much of it on the South Side:

Adams House (1900-01)	9326 S. Pleasant Ave.
American System-Built Houses (1917)	10410 and 10541 S. Hoyne Ave.
Bach House (1915)	7415 N. Sheridan Rd.
Foster House and Stable (1900)	12147 S. Harvard Ave.
Heller House (1897)	5132 S. Woodlawn Ave.
Roloson Houses (1894)	3213–19 S. Calumet Ave.
Waller Apartments (1895)	2840–48 W. Walnut St.
Walser House (1903)	42 N. Central Ave.

Jane Addams Hull-House Museum★

800 S. Halsted St., on the University of Illinois campus. From the Loop, drive west on W. Adams St. and turn south on Halsted St. 312-413-5353. www.uic.edu/jaddams/hull. Open year-round Tue–Fri 10am–4pm, Sun noon–4pm. Closed Mon, Sat & major holidays.

If you're interested in the history of immigration in Chicago, Hull House is for you. Founded in 1889 by pioneering social workers Jane Addams and Ellen Gates Starr, the settlement house became a focal point for citywide and national movements to improve living and working conditions of the nation's poor and disadvantaged.

Observing similar work in London in 1886, twenty-six-year-old Addams returned to Chicago inspired. In 1889 she and Starr moved into a Near West Side neighborhood teeming with immigrant families (the house they occupied was built in 1856 by real-estate developer Charles Hull). Through their dedication to helping the poor, and their aggressive agenda of education, social service and reform, Hull-House grew to a complex of 13 buildings—including Chicago's first public gymnasium, art and music schools and a cooperative residence for working women. Today only the house and the Residents' Dining Hall remain, renovated and converted into a museum. The house itself is furnished in the Victorian style with many original pieces, including Jane Addams' desk.

Mediterranean Dining on the West Side

If your visit to Hull House makes you hungry, never fear. Just north over the expressway, the city's best Greek eateries line South Halsted Street. For Greek-style hospitality, seafood, fresh lamb—and, of course, *saganaki* (pan-fried kasseri cheese that's flamed with brandy—opa!), it's hard to go wrong here. **Greek Islands** *(200 S. Halsted St.; 312-782-9855)* is typically boisterous; across the street, charmingly rustic **Santorini** *(800 W. Adams St.; 312-829-8820)* emphasizes seafood. On summer evenings, stop for appetizers or dessert on the outdoor roof garden at **Pegasus** *(130 S. Halsted St.; 312-226-4666)*.

If Italian dining is more your style, head for **Little Italy**, and especially the restaurants lining Taylor Street between Ashland and Halsted streets. From cozy cucinas like **RoSal's** *(1154 W. Taylor St.; 312-243-2357)*, to the upscale **Tuscany** *(1014 W. Taylor St.; 312-829-1990)*, this neighborhood brims with good food. For the truest neighborhood atmosphere, try no-frills **Tufano's Vernon Park Tap** *(1073 W. Vernon Park Pl.; 312-733-3393; cash only)*, where Southern Italian dishes are served family style and the classic Chicago bar buzzes with activity.

Prairie Avenue Historic District★

Drive south from the Loop on Michigan Ave., turn left at 18th St. and continue two blocks to Prairie Ave. (no through traffic). www.cityofchicago/Landmarks/P/PrairieAveDistrict.html.

The area south of downtown ranks today among the hippest, fastest-growing residential sections of the city. Though it seems like a modern phenomenon, it all started along Prairie Avenue after the Chicago Fire in 1871. Here on "Millionaire's Row" lived industrial and commercial leaders Marshall Field and George Pullman, among others, in mansions designed by famous architects such as Richard Morris Hunt, Burnham & Root and Henry Hobson Richardson. For a while, Prairie Avenue was the city's most fashionable address, but families moved to the North Side as industry invaded the neighborhood after 1900. In contrast, State Street between 16th and 22nd streets became the notorious Levee, an area of saloons and brothels. By 1966 industrial growth had caused the demolition of most of Prairie Avenue's mansions; a Chicago Landmark District was created in 1979 to preserve the remaining homes.

While You're in the Neighborhood . . .

Around the corner from Glessner House, the **National Vietnam Veterans Art Museum** exhibits a powerful collection of works by veterans of the war in Southeast Asia *(1801 S. Indiana Ave.; 312-326-0270; www.nvvam.org; not recommended for children)*. Once the Chess Records Studio, famous for recording Muddy Waters, Howlin' Wolf, Chuck Berry and other blues greats, **Blues Heaven** *(2120 S. Michigan Ave; 312-808-1286; www.bluesheaven.com)* now houses a foundation created to document the blues and to support blues artists *(studio tours Mon–Fri noon–3pm, Sat noon–2pm)*.

House Museums

Two of the city's most historically significant house museums form the district's core. One-hour tours of either or both *(312-326-1480; www.glessner house.org; open year-round Wed–Sun noon–3pm; closed major holidays; $10 each or $15 for both)* begin at the coach house of Glessner House. Tours of the neighborhood are offered on alternating Sundays from July to September.

John Jacob Glessner House★★ – *1800 S. Prairie Ave.* Designed by H.H. Richardson in 1886, the Glessner House revolutionized domestic American architecture with its open floor plan and plain facade. John Glessner, a manufacturer of farm implements, commissioned the house at a time when labor unrest alarmed the city's wealthy residents. In response, the architect designed the mansion like a fortress by turning

its back to the street and including a secure inner courtyard.

Henry B. Clarke House★ – *1855 S. Indiana Ave.* Built in 1836 for New York merchant Henry Clarke in the Greek Revival style (notice the heavy columns on the front porch), this white clapboard home is considered Chicago's oldest structure. It was moved here in 1977 from South Wabash Avenue.

Pullman Historic District★

Between 107th & 115th Sts. along Cottage Grove Ave. 773-785-8901. www.pullmanil.org.

Located in an industrial district on the Far South Side, this fascinating community was created by railroad-car magnate **George Pullman**—famous for his luxurious train coaches—in 1881 as an experimental company town. He incorporated the Pullman Palace Car Company in 1867, but 10 years later striking rail workers shocked the nation and open conflict between labor and management threatened. Wishing to isolate his employees from the strike- and strife-prone city, Pullman built his new factory town on 500 acres 13 miles south of Chicago. He hired architect Solon Beman and landscaper Nathan F. Barrett to design the factories and a com-

prehensive town plan. Pullman ran his "perfect town" for a profit, collecting rents from workers and providing services and necessities. Ever the capitalist, Pullman maintained ownership of all the property in his community; he set rents and refused to let anyone own individual houses. But economic depression in the 1890s brought wage cuts, and to keep the town profitable, Pullman raised rents and food prices. The company's employees rebelled, and strikes and bloody conflict led to the end of Pullman's plan. In 1971 the town was listed on the National Register of Historic Places; its restoration continues today.

Touring Tips

Pullman is located about 13 miles south of the Loop. To get there by car, drive south on I-94 and exit at 111th Street westbound (Exit 66A). The Pullman Historic District is four blocks west of the expressway. To get there by train, take the Metra Electric District Line from the Randolph Street Metra Station; exit at 111th Street *(fare and schedule information: 312-836-7000; www.metrarail.com).*

Begin your visit at the **Historic Pullman Foundation Visitor Center** *(11141 S. Cottage Grove Ave., entrance on 112th St. side; open year-round Tue–Sun 11am–2pm; closed Mon & major holidays),* which features a video presentation and exhibits, and stocks maps and brochures. Guided walking tours depart from the visitor center on the first Sunday of the month *(May–Oct 1:30pm–3:30pm).* A number of historic homes are open for viewing the second weekend in October for the **Annual Pullman House Tour** *(11am–5pm; $18 at the door, $15 in advance).* On the tour, you'll see a cross-section of private Pullman residences, from ornate mansions to simple workers' cottages and multi-unit apartments.

A Walk Through the District

After years of neglect, the community was lovingly restored and today is best sampled by a stroll down the 19C streets. A variety of Victorian residences fill the 16 blocks of the South Pullman residential district. The larger homes of managers face 111th Street, while smaller row houses and double houses of craftsmen and workers line the streets south to 115th Street. Varied and picturesque rooflines are typical of the Queen Anne style so popular among Victorian architects (but more often seen on larger houses). Architect Solon Beman also designed the simpler homes of North Pullman *(between 104th & 108th Sts.)* for workers of two other factories; the most charming stretch runs along Cottage Grove Avenue at 107th Street, where the houses are staggered along the angling thoroughfares. Though it's closed for restoration, you can still see the exterior of the **Hotel Florence** *(1111 S. Forestville Ave.)*—named for Pullman's daughter—which was off-limits to workers and where only visiting businessmen were allowed to drink.

Rest in Peace

Pullman's social experiment did not end well, and employees turned on him in anger when he lowered wages but refused to lower rents. When he died in 1897, his family was so worried that his grave in Graceland Cemetery would be robbed that they covered the coffin in tar paper and asphalt, sealing it into a concrete block. Railroad ties were used to overlay and safeguard the tomb further. As far as we know, the sleeping-car prince still rests securely in peace.

Residents of "The City of Big Shoulders" may work hard, but they play hard, too. Chicagoans have a great sense of fun, and they love to share it with visitors. What else would you expect from the folks who brought you The Second City *(see Nightlife)*, the Ferris wheel and the Tootsie Roll? So go ahead, have some fun, Chicago style.

Navy Pier★★

600 E. Grand Ave. at Lake Michigan. 312-595-7437. www.navypier.com. Open May–Aug Sun–Thu 10am–10pm, Fri–Sat 10am–midnight. Sept–Oct & Apr–May Sun–Thu 10am–8pm, Fri–Sat 10am–10pm. Nov–Mar Mon–Thu 10am–8pm, Fri–Sat 10am–10pm, Sun 10am–7pm. Attractions have separate admission fees. Shops & restaurants closed Thanksgiving Day & Dec 25.

Navy Pier has enjoyed many lives since it was first built in 1916 as—you guessed it—a passenger and freight terminal. Then it served as a naval training station during World War II and as a campus for the University of Illinois. It has hosted festivals, conventions and trade shows. After a period of disuse, the pier was reborn in 1995 as the colorful, bustling and thoroughly touristy place you see today. Many of Chicago's sightseeing cruise ships come and go from here, giving the place a truly nautical atmosphere.

In its 50 acres, the pier offers something for everyone, from high culture (the excellent Shakespeare Theater; *see Performing Arts*) to carnival food and fun. If it's raining, duck indoors to the **IMAX Theater** or shop for that perfect souvenir. Relax amid the palms in the tropical **Crystal Gardens** or grab a bite at one of many eateries *(see sidebar opposite)*. Outdoors, the 150-foot **Ferris wheel** beckons, or how about miniature golf with a Chicago theme?

Touring Tip

If you do nothing else, take a walk to the end of the 3,000-foot-long pier for some great skyline and lake **views★★**. On summer Saturdays and Wednesdays, fireworks light up the night sky over the pier *(starting at 9:30pm)*. See Musts for Kids for an array of Navy Pier's kid stuff. For information about getting to Navy Pier, see p 13.

Chicago Children's Museum★ – *On Navy Pier. See Musts for Kids.*

Smith Museum of Stained-Glass Windows ★ – *On Navy Pier. See Museums.*

Gourmet to Grub: Dining at the Pier

Though the fare here is definitely touristy and on the pricey side, you'll find a good variety of styles and lots of kid-friendly food. Navy Pier is among the few venues in the city for waterfront dining, and many places have both indoor and outdoor seating. Lively **Joe's Be-Bop Café & Jazz Emporium** *(312-595-5299)* serves up southern barbecue and traditional live jazz every night (there may be a cover charge). And **Bubba Gump Shrimp Co. & Market** features, well, shrimp and a lot of artificial "atmosphere" *(312-252-4867; www.bubbagump.com)*. On the quieter side, **Charlie's Ale House** offers pub surroundings, complete with 70 beers and a list of single-malt scotches, as well as a family-friendly menu *(312-595-1440)*. For fast food, head to the food court, McDonald's, the beer garden (with free live music) or the **Haagen Dazs Café** for sandwiches and oh-so-rich ice cream. You'll find terrific upscale seafood, steak and pasta at **Riva,** which also offers more casual dining at its first-level bar *(312-644-7482)*.

Attend a TV Show Taping

You have your choice: Jerry Springer or Oprah Winfrey. Both are taped in Chicago. Tickets are free, but you must plan ahead to join the studio audience for either of these talk shows, and you must be 18 years of age. Tapings generally take place twice on scheduled days during the taping season. Here's the scoop:

Oprah Winfrey Show – *312-591-9222 or www.oprah.com.* Reservations are taken only about a month in advance. Shows are taped August through November and January through May, though days vary week to week. Occasionally, you can snag last-minute tickets by email, so check the Web site.

Jerry Springer Show – *312-321-5365 or www.jerryspringertv.com.* Shows are taped September through April on Monday, Tuesday and Wednesday, except during weeks of major holidays. You can also get tickets by mail by writing to the studio at 454 N. Columbus Drive, 2nd Floor, Chicago, IL 60611.

Catch a Cubs Game at Wrigley Field

1060 W. Addison St., at Clark St. From downtown, take Lake Shore Dr. north and turn left on Irving Park Rd.; then go west on Clark St. 773-404-2827. http://chicago.cubs.mlb.com.

Sure, there are a lot of sporting events you could enjoy in Chicago, but there's only one **Wrigley Field★** *(see Landmarks)*. Nestled into a busy residential neighborhood on Chicago's North Side, the field languishes sleepily until baseball season when the joint really starts jumping. Cubs' games sell out quickly; in February the team announces the method by which tickets will be sold (in 2004 buyers were issued wristbands determining their place in line).

During the season, fans jam neighborhood streets and bars for hours before and after each game. The park seats just over 39,000; seating on the rooftops of neighboring buildings can be reserved for groups *(www.ballparkroof tops.com)*. If you can't get into a game, try one of the ballpark tours offered on Saturdays and Sundays during baseball season (no tours on game days; purchase tickets in advance). And don't forget about the White Sox, who play at U.S. Cellular Field *(333 W. 35th St.; 312-674-1000; www.chisox.com)*.

Getting Tickets Before You Come

Individual Cubs' game tickets generally go on sale in late February for the season ahead. To find out when tickets are available and how to purchase them, go to *http://chicago.cubs.mlb.com* and click on tickets, or call 773-404-2827. When tickets are released, you can purchase them online at the Cubs' Web site *(above)* or at *www.tickets.com (call 800-843-2827 in Illinois, or 866-652-2827 outside Illinois)*. Be prepared—there may be a limit to the number of tickets you can buy, and be patient; getting through by phone or email can be difficult.

If You Strike Out . . .

There's more local baseball to enjoy:

Chicago White Sox – American League, Chicago. *312-674-1000 or 866-769-4263. www.chisox.com.*

Kane County Cougars – Class A Affiliate of the Oakland Raiders, Midwest League. *630-232-8811. www.kccougers.com.*

Joliet JackHammers – Independent minor league, Northern League. *815-725-2255. www.jackhammerbaseball.com.*

Milwaukee Brewers – National League, Milwaukee. *414-902-4100. www.milwaukee. brewers.mlb.com.*

Take a Tour

Chicago offers a wealth of different tours for every taste. Here's a sampling:

Untouchable Tours – *773-881-1195. www.gangstertour.com. Tours depart from the corner of Clark & Ohio Sts., year-round daily 10am; additional tours Thu–Sun 1pm, Fri 7:30pm & Sat 5pm. $24.* No image of Chicago is more popular,

or enduring, than the city as a hotbed of gangsters. Even though Al Capone and his cronies are long gone, you can still tour the notable and notorious landmarks of hoodlumdom, including the site of the St. Valentine's Day massacre, and the Biograph Theater, where John Dillinger was shot. Costumed guides conduct these two-hour bus tours in character for a light-hearted look at Prohibition-era Chicago.

Chicago Neighborhood Tours – *312-742-1190. www.chgocitytours.com. Tours depart from the Chicago Cultural Center, 77 W. Randolph St. Reservations required. $25, includes refreshments.* One good way to explore some of the Windy City's more than 130 neighborhoods is on a Chicago Neighborhood Tour, offered by the City of Chicago. Visit historic **Bronzeville** and the South Side, the soul of Chicago's African-American community, or **Uptown**, home of the city's oldest jazz club. Or discover the ethnic flavors of enclaves like Little Italy, Greektown or Chinatown. Each tour is offered only a few times a year, so check the schedule before you go.

Chicago River Tours – *See p 38.*

Festival Fun at the Lake

The temperature isn't the only thing that's cooler by Lake Michigan. The annual **4th of July party** (held the evening of July 3) along the downtown lakefront attracts over a million people, making it the largest such celebration in the US; the spectacular fireworks show, set off from barges just outside Monroe Street Harbor, starts at 9:30pm. The city celebrates **Venetian Night** in late July with a parade of decorated and illuminated vessels in Monroe Harbor *(8:30pm)*, followed by fireworks over the water set to rock music broadcast on WXRT (93FM). The **Chicago Air and Water Show** attracts 2 million gawkers over one weekend in August to see the daredevil jet-powered Thunderbirds and other acrobatic stunt flyers duck and dodge high rises at incredible speeds. It's free, but crowded along the Near North Side beaches, the center of the action. For all these events, leave the car and take public transportation, or expect long waits in traffic. *For more information, check online at www.cityof chicago.org/specialevents.*

With beaches along Lake Michigan and green spaces galore, Chicago claims plenty of places to play outdoors. So grab your bike, your volleyball, your golf clubs or your ice skates—whatever the season, you won't run out of things to do.

Outdoor Fun in Millennium Park★★★

Bounded by Michigan Ave., Randolph & Monroe Sts. and Columbus Dr. 312-742-1168. www.millenniumpark.org. Open year-round daily 6am–11pm. See Parks and Gardens.

Arriving by bike? Park it, at no charge, at the **Bicycle Station** *(239 E. Randolph St.; 888-245-3929).* Or purchase a daily pass *($10 for 10 days)* for secure parking and access to showers and lockers. During summer festivals and music events, valet bike parking is free! The Bicycle Station also rents bikes by the hour, day or week, and there's even an on-site repair shop and snack bar. Guided bike/walk tours are offered daily in summer *(10am & 1pm).*

For wintertime fun in the park, try out those figure-eights at the **McCormick Tribune Ice Rink** *(opposite).*

Park Grill

11 N. Michigan Ave. 312-521-7275. www.theparkgrill.com.

For that après-skate dinner, try the rinkside Park Grill, a wood-trimmed, white-tablecloth restaurant serving an upscale American menu. During the summer, the Grill expands into Chicago's largest alfresco-dining venue. You can also reserve picnic bags to go.

Beach It★★

Along the lakefront from 7600 Sheridan Rd., at Howard St., to 9500 E. Ewing Ave., at Calumet Beach. 312-747-0832. www.chicagoparkdistrict.com.

Okay, it's not the Riviera, but Chicago's beaches are sandy, sunny and beautiful. Over 30 of them line the lakefront from north to south, and lifeguards are on duty from Memorial Day to Labor Day *(9am–9:30pm).* Some, like the Rogers Park beaches at the north end of the city, are no bigger than a block wide. Others, such as North Avenue Beach and 63rd Street Beach, have bathhouses, concessions and other amenities as well as large stretches of sand. Several beaches feature nature trails, others have tennis courts and volleyball set-ups. The best sands to see and be seen? That would be **Oak Street Beach** *(access via tunnels at Oak or Division Sts.),* where the tanned and toned soak up rays and swim in the shadow of the Drake Hotel *(see Neighborhoods).*

Touring Tip

Lake Michigan can be cold, especially in the spring, but the swimming is pleasant and refreshing. If swimming is restricted because of high bacteria counts in the water, lifeguards will post warning signs.

Go Skate

Chicago's long, cold winter has some good points: it sets the scene for some great ice-skating opportunities. The city has nine out-door rinks *(open late Nov–late Feb)* where you can practice your double axels. We've listed a couple below *(for a complete list of ice-skating rinks and in-line skate parks, contact the Chicago Park District: 312-742-7529 or www.chicagoparkdistrict.com).*

- **McCormick Tribune Ice Rink at Millennium Park** – *Michigan Ave. between Washington & Madison Sts. 312-742-5222. Open daily 10am–10pm.* Bring your own blades and skate free of charge, or rent skates *($7).*

- **Daley Bicentennial Plaza** – *337 E. Randolph St., in the Loop. 312-742-7650. Open Mon–Fri 10am–3:30pm & 7pm–9pm, weekends 8:30am–noon. $2 adults, $1 children under age 14. Skate rentals $2 adults, $1 children.*

Gotta grind? Crave a carve? Check out one of Chicago's two permanent street skateparks: 20,000 square feet each of fast concrete fit for old- and new-school skaters alike:

- **Wilson Skatepark** – *Wilson Ave. & Lake Shore Dr.*

- **Burnham Skatepark** – *31st St. & Lake Shore Dr.*

Hit the Links

Chicago Park District courses: 312-245-0909. www.cpdgolf.com. Open year-round (weather permitting) daily dawn to dusk.

Golf? In Chicago? You bet, so don't forget your clubs! The Chicago Park District has six courses, three driving ranges *(open 7am–10pm)*, two miniature-golf courses and three learning centers spread all around the city. Five of the courses are nine-hole; the sixth, at Jackson Park, is a full 18 holes. Daily fees vary from $10 to $21 (slightly higher on weekends) and tee times can be re-served online or by phone. Beautiful lake views, at Marovitz on the North Side and Jackson Park and the South Shore Cultural Center on the South Side, will no doubt improve your game. *For a list of courses and details, check online at www.cpdgolf.com or www.kempersports.com.*

The Green: Putting in Grant Park

Tucked away in an old bus turnaround on Monroe Drive between Lake Shore Drive and Columbus Avenue, this new 18-hole putting course features lush plantings, great views and downtown convenience. At par 42, it offers players a chance to practice their short game with a true-golf experience. It's fun for beginners, too. Enjoy lunch, dinner or snack at The Green's full-service patio restaurant. Call for reservations and tee-times *(352 E. Monroe St.; 312-642-7888; www.thegreenonline.com).*

Okay, you've done the architecture, the museums and the historic sites. Now what about the kids? Or the kid in you? Here are some Chicago spots the whole family can enjoy.

Art Institute of Chicago★★★

111 S. Michigan Ave. 312-443-3600. www.artic.edu/aic. See Museums.

Begin your family visit to the AIC on the lower level in the **Kraft Education Center,** where kids are invited to get up close and personal with art. Drop-in workshops and craft programs are offered, and the museum also fills a calendar with children's events that require pre-registration. In the **Touch Gallery**, you can do just that, which is, of course, strictly forbidden elsewhere in the museum. Next door, explore the **Thorne Miniature Rooms★★**, tiny handcrafted rooms from 68 periods and places around the world. Like fancy dollhouses, each room is furnished on a scale of 1 inch to 1 foot, right down to the rugs and silverware. Up one flight, in the long hall that connects the museum's two wings, fans of long ago and far away will dig displays of arms and armor, swords and scabbards.

> **Touring Tip**
>
> To prepare for a visit to the Art Institute with children, check out the museum's Web site *(above)* for activities and suggestions on how the kids can have fun with art.

Field Museum of Natural History★★★

1400 S. Lake Shore Dr. 312-922-9410. www.fieldmuseum.org. See Museums.

Dinos and mummies and bugs, oh my! What more could a kid want? Though much of this museum is geared for older kids and adults, there are some notable highlights for younger visitors—**Sue★★**, the 47-foot-long T-rex, topping the list. For more prehistoric beasts, head to the upper level of the East Wing, where the **DinoZone★★** exhibit will delight with skeletons of long-necked *Apatasauras*, horned *Triceratops* and the winged *Pteranodon*. On the ground level, **Underground Adventure★** simulates the dark, creepy-crawly world beneath our feet. Your young ones may also enjoy **What Is an Animal?** and **Inside Ancient Egypt**. Of course, kids with special interests in nature and animals could spend all day at the Field.

John G. Shedd Aquarium★★★

1200 S. Lake Shore Dr. 312-559-0200. www.shedd.org. See Museums.

This place is a winner with kids of all ages. Brightly colored sea creatures captivate little ones, while bigger kids focus on sharks and piranhas and octopi. As you enter, check in the Kovler Family Hall for locations of **Animal Encounters** *(daily 11:30am & 2:30 pm)*, where kids go one-on-one with snakes, tarantulas or frogs. On Tuesdays, you'll find events for preschoolers (ages 3-5) posted there as part of the **Tots on Tuesdays** program, which includes story times, crafts, animal touch programs, music, and characters in costume. And, of course, neither you nor the kids will want to miss the **Marine Mammal Presentations** in the **Oceanarium**★★ or feeding time at the **Caribbean Reef**★.

Hooray for Kayavak!

As you visit the Oceanarium, keep your eyes peeled for Kayavak, a very special beluga whale. You'll know her by the white birthmark on her back. The little whale's mother died of an infection when Kayavak was only five months old. Because the calf was still nursing, this might have meant certain death for her, too. But keepers at the aquarium were determined to keep Kayavak alive. They weaned her immediately to solid food (fish), hoping that she'd be able to make the transition. At least two human companions remained with her 24/7 for the next year, swimming with her 30 minutes of each hour. All night and all day, they fed and played with her, watching her grow strong and healthy. When the time finally came to introduce her to the other whales, they refused to accept her, chasing her away and even beating her up. The scene was painful for the keepers to watch, but absolutely necessary if Kayavak was to live as a normal beluga. One morning, the trainers arrived to find Kayavak swimming together with the pod. Now five years old, she still ranks lowest in the whale hierarchy, but she's tough and feisty and gets along fine.

Museum of Science and Industry★★★

57th St. at S. Lake Shore Dr. From downtown, take Lake Shore Dr. south and turn right on 57th St. 773-684-1414. www.msichicago.org. Open year-round Memorial Day–Labor Day, Mon–Sat 9:30am–5:30pm, Sun 11am–5:30pm. Rest of the year Mon–Sat 9:30am–4pm, Sun 11am–4pm. Closed Dec 25. $9 adults, $5 children, ages 3-11 (free admission Mon). Additional charge for Omnimax Theater & special exhibits. By bus, take the #6 Jackson Park Express bus south to 56th St. and walk 1 block south. In summer, the #10 MSI bus runs right to the museum. Or take Metra train to 57th St. Station and walk east 2 blocks.

There's a lot here for kids—and adults—to love, and we mean a lot. Here are some of the most popular kid stops. *For more on the MSI, see Museums.*

Musts at the MSI

Coal Mine★★ – *Main floor*. A favorite here since 1933, this 20-minute guided tour plunges you from the top of the "headframe" to the "depths" (only a floor down) of a replica coal mine by elevator.

Imaging: Tools of Science★★ – *Main floor*. Computers invite you to manipulate images of your face, create art and solve crimes.

Toymaker 3000★★ – The best part about this exhibit, intended to teach kids how to create and run a business, is watching a 2,000-square-foot robotic assembly line manufacture 300 tops an hour.

Fairy Castle★ – Furnished with over 1,000 miniatures, the jewel-encrusted Fairy Castle even has running water and electricity. The castle is chock-full of references to familiar fairy tales. Can you find the Bluebird of Happiness?

Heart Balcony★ – Withstanding the test of time since 1952, the exhibit's 16-foot-tall Walk-Through Heart shows how the beat goes on within us. The heart now forms the centerpiece for an updated exhibit on cardiac health.

U-505 Submarine★ – Closed until the spring of 2005, the submarine is being reinstalled and enclosed in the northeast corner of the museum. The new 35,000-square-foot exhibit will allow you to see the sub's exterior up close.

All Hands On!

Kids love to climb, and MSI has plenty of things for little ones to clamber on. In **Ships Through the Ages,** kids can man the wheel of a 19C tall ship. To experience liftoff, climb aboard the model **space shuttle** in the Henry Crown Space Center; and for a realistic flight experience, brave the F-14 Tomcat simulators in **Navy: Technology at Sea★** on the main floor. In **Petroleum Planet**, you can even "drive" racecars.

Transportation Zone★ – You'll find many of the museum's large vehicles on the main floor, including a cutaway of an actual **Boeing 727★**. The newest star of the gallery is **The Great Train Story★**, where model trains chug around a 3,500-square-foot layout that simulates the busy rail commerce between Chicago and Seattle. Be sure to stop at **All Aboard the Silver Streak★** on the ground floor as you leave for a tour of the **Pioneer Zephyr**, the sleek passenger train that took the West by storm from 1934 to 1960.

Chick Hatchery – Young and old alike are fascinated by watching baby chicks peck their way out of the egg. Part of the exhibit, Genetics–Decoding Life, the Chick Hatchery is located on the main floor, next to the Transportation Zone.

Idea Factory – *Ground floor; entry by free timed tickets are available at the exhibit entrance.* Very young kids will enjoy this 8,000-square-foot area, loaded with toys and tools for a good time, including a fabulous moat that encircles the space. Next door, 22,000 hand-carved miniature mechanical figures make their way around the **Circus** exhibit.

Henry Crown Space Center – Home of the **Omnimax Theater** *(purchase advance tickets online or by calling the museum)*, this wing also houses the **Apollo 8 command module★**, the first spacecraft ever to circle the moon (1968).

Finnegan's Ice Cream Parlor

If you happen to wander down **Yesterday's Main Street** on the main floor behind the Coal Mine, you might want to "set a spell" at **Finnegan's**. Based on a South Side soda fountain popular in 1917, it serves ice-cream concoctions, sandwiches and Starbucks coffee. Main Street itself was installed in 1943, a return to the "good old days" of 1910 intended to take people's minds off World War II.

Navy Pier★★ for Kids

600 E. Grand Ave. at Lake Michigan. See Landmarks. For information about free trolleys to Navy Pier, see p 13.

If you can keep them out of the candy and ice-cream shops, Navy Pier has rides and amusements that will entertain kids for hours. It won't be cheap, though—each attraction charges its own admission fee. The **Ferris wheel**, a pier landmark, soars up 150 feet, but for more excitement, the **Wave Swinger** slings riders through the air. For young kids, there's the old-fashioned **carousel** with its 36 colorful animals. For some really cheesy fun, try Amazing Chicago's Funhouse Maze or the Time Escape 3D Ride, both of which use special effects to transport you through Chicago as you'll never see it again. The Pier also features a mini-golf course and a Build-A-Bear Workshop, for making stuffed animals.

Chicago Children's Museum★ – *312-527-1000. www.chichildrensmuseum.org. Open year round daily 10am–5pm (Thu until 8pm). Closed Thanksgiving Day & Dec 25. $7. Free admission Thu after 5pm.*

The Children's Museum greets visitors as they enter Navy Pier on foot. There's lots to do here for the under-11-year-old set. Three floors of hands-on exhibits invite youngsters to build bridges and forts, invent a flying machine, dig up dinosaur bones, meet giant insects, explore a replica schooner, and even appear on TV. Programs, performances and workshops (along with happy kids) make this museum a lively place.

Theater for Kids

These Chicago theaters love kids and kids love them back.

Chicago Kids Company – *773-205-9600. www.chicagokidscompany.com.* The company puts on fun plays for kids at various venues.

Emerald City Theatre Company – *773-529-2690. www.emeraldcitytheatre.com.* Emerald City offers Cinderella, Wizard of Oz and the like, mostly performed at the Apollo Theater.

Lifeline Theatre – *6912 N. Glenwood Ave. 773-761-4477. www.lifelinetheatre.com.* This small neighborhood theater stages great adult plays, too.

Puppet Parlor – *1922 W. Montrose Ave. 773-774-2919.* Puppet Parlor is Chicago's only marionette theater for kids.

Vittum Theater – *1012 N. Noble St. 773-342-4141. www.vittumtheater.org.* Serious and comic theater performances here are tailored to young audiences.

Brookfield Zoo★★

8400 W. 31st St., Brookfield. 14mi west of Chicago. 708-485-0263. www.brookfieldzoo.org. Open Memorial Day–Labor Day daily 9:30am–6pm. Rest of the year daily 10am–5pm. $8 adults, $4 children ages 3-11. Free admission Tue & Thu Oct–Mar.

If you have a day to spend, it's worth the jaunt to this suburban zoo. Its 216 acres fan out around a central fountain, and 15 miles of footpaths wind through the lovely grounds. Shady stretches of lawn invite picnicking. With over 2,800 resident beasts, you'll find all your favorites here, from aardvarks to zebras. Here are several exhibits you, and the kids, won't want to miss.

Brookfield Breakdown

Seven Seas★★ – Make a bee-line in the morning for the Dolphinarium to see a **Dolphin Presentation★** *(several 20min performances daily; $2.50 adults, $2 children).* Later shows tend to get crowded.

Tropic World★★ – Inhabited by primates, this area offers a dramatic treetop perspective of life in the rain forests of Asia, Africa and South America.

The Fragile Kingdom★ – Clouded leopards, comical meerkats and naked mole rats occupy habitats that re-create an African desert and an Asian rain forest.

Habitat Africa!★ – Wander from the open savanna to the dense forest, with views of giraffes, okapis, crocodiles and pythons along the way.

Regenstein Wolf Woods – Brookfield's newest habitat, located in the south-western corner of the zoo, is home to a pack of endangered Mexican gray wolves. The pack is most active at the beginning and the end of the day.

Touring Tip

To get to the zoo by car from downtown, drive west on I-290 to the First Avenue exit, then continue south on 1st Avenue to 31st Street and follow signs to the main North Gate parking lot *($8)*. By train, take the Burlington Northern Metra train line from Union Station in the Loop. Get off at the zoo stop at Hollywood Station and walk north two blocks *(fares & schedules: 312-836-7000; www.metrarail.com).*

A good way to see the sprawling zoo is via the 45-minute **Motor Safari Tour** *($2.50 adults, $1.50 children)*; tickets are good for one round-trip ride, so you can take in all the zoo or get on and off at any of the four stops. Zoo eateries offer everything from hot dogs and pizza (Safari Stop, Ituri Café) to sit-down meals at Bocaditos. Health food? Try the Eco Café. Children's "Animeals" are available at many of the restaurants.

Lincoln Park Zoo★★

2200 N. Cannon Dr. 312-742-2000. www.lpzoo.org. Grounds open year-round daily 9am–6pm. Zoo buildings open year-round daily 10am–5pm. Memorial Day–Labor Day weekends and holidays grounds close 7pm, buildings close 6:30pm. Nov–Mar grounds close 5pm, buildings close 4:30pm.

In addition to its wonderful penguin and bird houses, bear and cat habitats and sea lion pool, this accessible zoo, convenient and free of charge, has updated several of its exhibits recently with an eye toward replicating environments and encouraging natural animal behavior. The completely remodeled **Pritzker Children's Zoo** opens in summer 2005 with a new theme: At Home in the Woods.

Lincoln Park Lineup

Regenstein Center for African Apes★★ – Gorillas and chimps cavort in their new 29,000-square-foot indoor-outdoor home. Watch them play on 5,000 feet of vines, fish for treats in "termite" mounds and scramble around the mud banks. Beware: they're watching you, too. They love to shoot bursts of air at visitors with a giant air gun!

Regenstein African Journey Pavilion★★ – There's a new habitat around every corner here, each one part of an African ecosystem—we dare you to step into a dark enclave filled with 10,000 Madagascar hissing cockroaches! Outdoors you can wander through the African savanna where the big guys—giraffes, elephants, ostriches—live, or take the **African Safari Ride** *($5)*. On the beautiful new **carousel** installed atop the education center, kids can ride their favorite endangered animals *($2; open Mar–Oct 10am–4:40pm)*.

Farm in the Zoo★ – At this renovated area, kids can climb aboard a tractor, meet the animals and feed and milk the cows *(check times)*.

Touring Tip

You can park for $12 along Cannon Drive to the east of the grounds *(enter from Fullerton Ave.)*. Pick up maps, audio tours or strollers in the **Gateway Pavilion** to the north of the main entrance off Cannon Drive. You might also find free parking in Lincoln Park along Stockton Drive to the zoo's west. CTA bus routes 151 and 156 both serve the zoo. If you want to ride around the zoo, hop aboard the **LPZOO Express** *($2)*.

Park Place Café offers good eats year-round in a food-court setting; or check out Big Cats, Landmark or Elephant cafes for quick bites in the warmer months. Step outside zoo boundaries to the south for a meal at historic **Café Brauer** *(see p 56)*.

American Girl Place

111 E. Chicago Ave. 877-247-5223. www.americangirl.com. Open year-round Mon–Wed 10am–7pm, Thu–Fri 9:30am–9pm, Sat 9am–9pm, Sun 9:30am–7pm. Closed Thanksgiving Day & Dec 25. Call for other seasonal hours.

Little girls and their dolls flock to this full-service fantasyland. After you shop the complete line of American Girl dolls and products (including dress-alike clothing for doll and child), the exhibits, cooking classes, theater programs and reading groups can keep you busy for the rest of the day *(many events require reservations)*. The cafe *(reservations recommended)* serves brunch, lunch, tea and dinner; special packages are available for birthday parties. Dolls can even have their hair done in the Doll Hair Salon. For little girls who love their dolls, AGP rocks. Try to catch a performance of *Circle of Friends, An American Girls Musical*.

ESPN Zone

43 E. Ohio St. 312-644-3776. www.espnzone.com/chicago. Open year-round Sun–Thu 11:30am–11pm, Fri 11:30am–midnight, Sat 11am–midnight.

Sports fans of all ages will revel in this digital-generation sports bar/arcade. On the second floor, the 10,000-square-foot Sports Arena offers tons of interactive sports and virtual-reality games ranging from bowling to car racing to skydiving. The third-floor Screening Room is equipped with a 16-foot, high-definition TV and surrounding monitors for the ultimate in multigame viewing.

City of the Big Pizzas

After a tough afternoon at the ESPN Zone, why not treat the kids to a Chicago-style pizza. The city ranks as one of the country's greatest spots for 'za; aficionados rave about the local deep-dish variety, sometimes called thick-crust or pan pizza. This savory concoction of tomatoes, cheese, sausage and vegetables ladled over a thick, doughy crust was developed in the 1940s by restaurateur Ike Sewell, whose restaurants **Pizzeria Uno** *(29 E. Ohio St.; 312-321-1000; www.pizzeriauno.com)* and, around the corner, **Pizzeria Due** *(619 N. Wabash St.; 312-943-2400; www.pizzeriauno.com)*, still serve the genuine article to crowds of eager eaters. (The difference? Due accommodates more people. Both menus are the same.) Be prepared to wait; cooking your massive pizza takes around 45 minutes. More than 2,000 restaurants in Chicago offer some permutation of this mouth-watering dish, with toppings ranging from mushrooms and pepperoni to clams and artichokes.

Must Go: Performing Arts

Chicago's theater and performing-arts scene is extraordinarily diverse and accomplished. With over 120 professional theater companies, Chicago offers everything from popular Broadway musicals to gritty "off-Loop" productions. Traditional and contemporary ethnic dance troupes and opera and ballet companies make their home here, and music of all kinds flows nightly. Here are some suggestions for a night at the theater.

Chicago Theater District

Many of the Loop's glorious 19C movie, vaudeville and stage theaters are gone now, but a few have been preserved and renovated, and new venues have been added. The theaters below are located throughout the Loop, but tend to cluster in the area bounded by Washington Street, Lake Street, LaSalle Street and Wabash Avenue. *Except where noted, you can purchase tickets for the Chicago Theater District venues online at: www.ticketmaster.com.*

Auditorium Theatre

50 E. Congress Pkwy. 312-922-2110. www.auditoriumtheatre.org.

The granddaddy of Chicago's historic theaters, this classic venue, which opened in 1889, makes for theatergoing at its best *(see Neighborhoods/Loop).* Its fine acoustics and lovely, renovated spaces are a delight. Programming varies from local dance troupes such as the Joffrey Ballet *(see p 82)* to Broadway musicals.

Cadillac Palace Theatre

151 W. Monroe St. 312-902-1400. www.broadwayinchicago.com.

This lavish venue, inspired by historic French palaces, started out in 1926 as a vaudeville house. It later featured both movies and live stage shows. Renovated and reopened in 1999, the Cadillac Palace now hosts pre-Broadway hits such as *The Producers* and other big-time musicals.

Chicago Theatre

175 N. State St. 312-462-6300. www.thechicagotheatre.com.

Opened as a movie palace in 1921, the glittering Chicago Theatre was resurrected, restored and reopened in 1986. Frank Sinatra performed the opening concert, and today the schedule ranges from Bonnie Raitt to the National Acrobats of Taiwan.

Touring Tip

For up-to-the-minute information and links to Chicago theaters and performing-arts organizations, check out the Web site of the League of Chicago Theatres: *www.theaterchicago.org.*

Gene Siskel Film Center

164 N. State St. 312-846-2600. www.siskelfilmcenter.org.

Founded in 1972 by the School of the Art Institute, the GSFC is a major center of cinematic art and history. The state-of-the-art facility screens new American and foreign films, independent productions and retrospectives.

Goodman Theatre

170 N. Dearborn St. 312-443-3800. www.goodman-theatre.org.

Long located adjacent to the Art Institute, the formidable Goodman Theatre moved in 2000 to this newly constructed home in the Loop. The theater still features classic and contemporary works of serious drama on its two stages.

Oriental Theatre/Ford Center for the Performing Arts

151 W. Randolph St. 312-902-1400. www.broadwayinchicago.com.

The "hasheesh-dream décor" of this 1926 theater that delighted silent-movie audiences has been restored for modern theatergoers. Large-scale stage productions such as *Ragtime*, *Fosse* and *Mamma Mia!* make a splash here.

Shubert Theatre

22 W. Monroe St. 312-902-1400. www.broadwayinchicago.com.

The Shubert was built as the Majestic Theatre, a popular vaudeville venue, in 1906. Along with box-office hits such as *Cabaret* and *Rent*, it's now known for such pre-Broadway engagements as *Sweet Smell of Success* starring John Lithgow, and *Movin' Out*, a collaboration by Twyla Tharp and Billy Joel.

Out of the Loop

Chicago's new **Millennium Park**★★★ *(see Parks and Gardens)* features two new performing-arts venues. Curling stainless-steel ribbons frame Frank Gehry's state-of-the-art **Jay Pritzker Pavilion**★★★, host to a variety of musical performances *(www.millen niumpark.org/events.htm)*. Opened in November 2003, the **Joan W. and Irving B. Harris Theater for Music and Dance** *(205 E. Randolph St.; 312-334-7777; www.madtchi.com)* provides a  much-needed home base for Chicago's midsize music and dance companies. The interior of this underground (literally) theater in Millennium Park may not be glitzy, but the sightlines and acoustics in the 1,500-seat space are excellent.

Other worthwhile venues outside the Loop include the 440-seat **Apollo Theater** *(2540 N. Lincoln Ave.; 773-935-6100; www.apollochicago.com)*, offering lighter musicals and stage works; and the **Athenaeum Theatre** *(2936 N. Southport Ave.; 773-935-6860; www.athenaeumtheatre.com)*, which stages dance, performance groups and theater schools from around the city in its 1,000-seat main stage.

Must Go: Performing Arts

Music and Dance

Chicago Symphony Orchestra

220 S. Michigan Ave. 312-294-3333. www.cso.org.

Over the last 112 years, the CSO has built a global reputation, which continues under the batons of Music Director Daniel Barenboim and Principal Guest Conductor Pierre Boulez. During the season *(Sept–June)*, barely a night goes by without music at the CSO's new Symphony Center.

Hubbard Street Dance Chicago

Various venues around Chicago. 312-850-9744. www.hubbardstreetdance.org.

For sheer athleticism and exuberance, the 21 dancers in Hubbard Street's main company can't be beat. With a repertoire that blends ballet, jazz, modern and ethnic dance and music into a seamless whole, these performances are always fun.

Joffrey Ballet

Auditorium Theatre, 50 E. Congress Pkwy. 312-739-0120. www.joffrey.com.

Still under the artistic direction of its co-founder (with Robert Joffrey), Gerald Arpino, the choreography and programming of this first-class dance company thrill audiences year-round.

Lyric Opera

20 N. Wacker Dr. 312-332-2244. www.lyricopera.org.

Chicago's major opera company occupies the stately Civic Opera House, which opened in 1929. The lavish theater seats over 3,500, and each season includes a classic or debuting American work.

Muntu Dance Theatre

Various venues around Chicago. 773-602-1135. www.muntu.com.

Founded in 1972, Muntu (which means the "essence of humanity" in Bantu) performs contemporary and historic African, Caribbean and African-American dance and music that pulse with rhythm and color.

Hot Tix

Try snagging half-price, same-day show tickets at one of the Hot Tix outlets *(www.hottix.org)* around the city: 78 W. Randolph St., Loop; 163 E. Pearson St., Magnificent Mile; 9501 N. Skokie Blvd., in Skokie; and at all Tower Records stores.

Chicago Theater Companies

Bailiwick Repertory Theatre

1229 W. Belmont Ave. 773-883-1090. www.bailiwick.org.

Anything goes here: from the raucous Naked Boys Singing to Shaw's *St. Joan*, you'll find it all at this theater. The Bailiwick Arts Center boasts a 150-seat main stage, a 90-seat studio and a 40-seat loft.

Chicago Shakespeare Theater

800 E. Grand Ave., on Navy Pier. 312-595-5600. www.chicagoshakes.com.

Shakespeare would love the carnival atmosphere of Navy Pier, where this delightful 500-seat courtyard theater stages marvelous interpretations of his works.

> **Touring Tip**
>
> Planning to attend a performance at the Shakespeare Theater? Make dinner reservations at **Riva** *(700 E. Grand Ave.; 312-644-7482; www.stefanirestaurants. com/riva.htm)* for a delicious pre-show meal with great lake and city views.

Steppenwolf Theatre

1650 N. Halsted St. 312-335-1650. www.steppenwolf.org.

You know their names: John Malkovich, Gary Sinise, William Peterson, Laurie Metcalf and so many others. They all did their early work at Steppenwolf, Chicago's premier off-Loop theater. The 510-seat Downstairs Theatre, the largest of three, features world premieres and new interpretations of the classics with a focus on the ensemble acting that made Steppenwolf famous. Upstairs and in the Garage Theater, emerging artists and new plays rule.

Victory Gardens Theatre

2257 N. Lincoln Ave. 773-871-3000. www.victorygardens.org.

Acclaimed for its productions of new and living playwrights, the VGT recently purchased the historic Biograph Theater (where gangster John Dillinger was shot), and plans to expand it into a five-theater complex. World premieres are a specialty here, so be the first on your block to see an exciting new work.

Ravinia Music Festival

200 Ravinia Park Rd., Highland Park. 847-266-5100. www.ravinia.org. This world-famous outdoor festival spreads out over 36 lush acres in the North Shore suburb of Highland Park. Summer home of the Chicago Symphony Orchestra since 1936, Ravinia today offers everything from jazz, pop and chamber music to folk, dance and children's programs. The complex includes several restaurants, covered pavilion seating, and two indoor theaters. Most fun, though, is to enjoy summertime performances with a picnic dinner on the lawn—with or without candelabra.

Forget any doubts you may have about Chicago's fashion sense: you can shop this town 'til you drop. Add a dose of midwestern good sense and practicality, a touch of the farm-fresh and a manageable scale, and you have a city where high-style boutiques rub elbows with bargain basements, vintage treasure troves and farmers' markets.

Magnificent Mile★★★

North Michigan Avenue is indisputably *the* shopping promenade in the city. As you stroll the lovely avenue from the river to **Oak Street★** *(opposite)*, you'll notice that Mag Mile has fallen victim to the homogenizing effect of contemporary retailing— chain stores like **Crate and Barrel**, **Williams-Sonoma**, **Banana Republic** and **Gap** now mingle with the exclusive boutiques. Even so, time spent shopping here will certainly not disappoint the acquisition-minded.

Who could resist tony Dallas retailer **Neiman Marcus** *(737 N. Michigan Ave.; 312-642-5900; www.neimanmarcus.com)*? Then there's **Filene's Basement** *(830 N. Michigan Ave.; 312-482-8918; www.filenesbasement. com)*, the country's oldest off-price department store; Swedish newcomer **H&M** *(840 N. Michigan Ave.; 312-640-0060; www.hm.com)*; and **Niketown Chicago** *(669 N. Michigan Ave.; 312-642-6363; www.niketown.nike.com)*, offering clothing for every sport.

Mag Mile Malls

Vertical malls add scores of stores and restaurants to the possibilities along North Michigan Avenue (malls below are listed from south to north).

Westfield North Bridge – *520 N. Michigan Ave. 312-327-2300. www.northbridgechicago.com*. Fifty shops and 30 restaurants fill this attractive mall, where the third floor is devoted exclusively to kids. This is the home of the Seattle retailer **Nordstrom**, which made the Chicago scene in 2000.

600 North Michigan Shops – *600 N. Michigan Ave. 312-266-5630*. Eddie Bauer is a highlight here, along with a multiplex movie theater.

Chicago Place – *700 N. Michigan Ave. 312-642-4811. www.chicago-place.com*. **Saks Fifth Avenue** anchors these eight levels, which include **Ann Taylor** and **Talbots**. Drop by delightful **Chiaroscuro**, a gallery of colorful, funky eclectica.

Water Tower Place★ – *835 N. Michigan Ave. 312-440-3166. www.shopwatertower.com*. Water Tower Place boasts the largest selection of all, from department-store chains Marshall Field and Lord & Taylor to trendy **Custo-Barcelona** and **#1 Blue Engine**, devoted exclusively to Thomas the Train.

900 North Michigan Shops – *900 N. Michigan Ave. 312-915-3916. www.shop900.com*. Swankest of the Mag Mile malls, 900 North Michigan includes **Bloomingdale's**, **Gucci** and **Lalique** among its 70 stores.

Magnificent Shopping Streets

Oak Street★ – *West side of Michigan Ave., one block north of Walton Pl.* Hunting for haute couture? Duck down Oak Street, where you'll flush out a wonderful array of designer boutiques, jewelry stores and intimate shops. Bag the hippest fashions at **Ultimo** *(no. 114; 312-787-1171; www.ultimo.com)* and **Prada** *(no. 30; 312-951-1113; www.prada.com)*, or shoot for quintessentially elegant accessories at **Hermès of Paris** *(no. 110; 312-787-8175; www.hermes.com)*. At **Frette** *(no. 41; 312-649-3744; www.frette.com)*, the high thread counts of the shop's fine Italian linens reflect equally high prices. Anchoring all this glamour is **Barneys New York** *(no. 25; 312-587-1700; www.barneys.com)*. Buyers beware: these trendy shops are not for the faint of budget.

State Street★ – *Between Randolph & Adams Sts.* Chicago's first retail corridor, State Street's fortunes in the Loop have soared and dipped over the years. That Great Street still offers two of Chicago's most famous homegrown retailers, the flagship **Marshall Field's★** *(111 N. State St.; see Neighborhoods)*, where "Give the lady what she wants" has long been the battle cry; and **Carson Pirie Scott★★★** *(1 S. State St.; see Neighborhoods)*, hailed for its architecture as well as its merchandise.

Armitage Avenue – *Between Halsted St. & Racine Ave.* Stroll this historic district, with its lovely residences, boutiques and eateries. Stop by **Tabula Tua** *(1015 W. Armitage Ave.; 773-525-3500; www.tabulatua.com)* for luscious table settings and other home accessories. Chicago women swear by **Lori's Designer Shoes** *(824 W. Armitage Ave.; 773-281-5655; www.lorisshoes.com)* for selection and price. And the jewelry at **Ancient Echoes** *(1022A W. Armitage Ave.; 773-880-1003; www.ancientechoes.com)* caters to those with a taste for the exotic. Parking here is tough; take public transportation if possible.

New Maxwell Street Market

Canal St. at Roosevelt Rd. Park for $3 at Clinton St. & 14th Pl. Open year-round Sun 7am–3pm. 312-922-3100. www.openair.org/oldmax/oldmax.html. Chicago's oldest outdoor market dates to the late 19C when Jewish immigrants ran a bustling open-air bazaar here. Although the market and its vendors and shoppers have changed over the years, the place always remained gritty and urban. Today, urban renewal has taken its toll, and the new, sanitized Maxwell Street Market is but a shadow of its former self. Still, more than 480 vendors peddle their wares—from produce to antiques—and street performers and musicians entertain.

Clark Street – *Between Foster & Bryn Mawr Aves.* Swedish in its origins, **Andersonville** has grown popular and eclectic in its shopping opportunities; you'll find antiques, home accessories and gifts here. For a Scandinavian fix, drop by the gift shop at the **Swedish-American Museum Center** *(5211 N. Clark St.; 773-728-8111; www.samac.org)*, loaded with Kosta Boda crystal and other Swedish specialties.

Damen Avenue – *From 1600 North.* Much of the trendy retail action of artsy **Bucktown** happens along Damen Avenue. Try **p.45** *(1643 N. Damen Ave.; 773-862-4523; www.p45.com)* for edgy women's fashion from Chicago's best young designers.

Devon Avenue – *Between Western & California Aves.* The "Midwest capital of gold dealers" contains nearly 20 jewelers selling mostly 22- and 24-karat gold jewelry. Bisecting the heart of Chicago's Indian and Jewish communities, Devon also features Indian restaurants and sari shops to the east, and farther west, purveyors of all things Judaica.

Division Street – *Especially the 1900 block.* Boutiques and funky shops line the main thoroughfare of Chicago's other hip young neighborhood, **Wicker Park**.

Wentworth Avenue – *South of Cermak Rd., in Chinatown.* A wonderful place to while away the afternoon, Chicago's **Chinatown** offers shops, groceries, bakeries and restaurants aplenty. Stores carry the usual interesting mix of American, Chinese and Japanese goods, including silk bathrobes, jackets and traditional dresses, ceramics and toys. **Woks 'n Things** *(2234 S. Wentworth Ave.; 312-842-0701)* stocks an amazing array of cookware. Be sure to roam the blocks west of Wentworth for more shops.

Farmers' Markets

Chicago prides itself on its neighborhood farmers' markets, which bring the bounty of the surrounding countryside into the city from May through October *(check online at www.egov.cityofchicago.org for times and locations)*.

Foodies should check out **Chicago's Green City Market** *(1750 N. Clark St., at Stockton Dr., in Lincoln Park; open mid-May–Oct Wed 7am–1pm; 847-835-2240; www.chicagogreencitymarket.org)*. This nonprofit market was created to support the sustainable and organic food movements in Chicago and to provide fresh local produce to an increasing number of restaurateurs. Operating since 1999, the Green Market is open to the public and features at least 50 vendors of heirloom fruits and vegetables along with cooking demonstrations by prominent local chefs.

River North Galleries

The **River North Gallery District** *(bounded on the east and west by N. Wells & N. Orleans Sts., and on the south and north by W. Huron St. & W. Chicago Ave.)* vies with Manhattan's Soho for claiming the largest concentration of art galleries. Clustered along and around Superior Street, galleries, antique shops and home-furnishings stores—many of which occupy 19C warehouses—provide the perfect setting to find that piece of art that you just can't live without.

On certain Friday evenings each month, galleries open their new shows *(for schedules check online at www.chicagogallerynews.com or pick up a free copy of Chicago Gallery News)*. If you're adding to your contemporary art collection, here's a few galleries to get you started:

Andrew Bae Gallery – *300 W. Superior St. 312-335-8601. www.andrewbae.com.* Andrew Bae specializes in contemporary and young Asian artists.

Carl Hammer Gallery – *740 N. Wells St. 312-266-8512. www.hammergallery.com.* "Outsider" and self-taught artists are featured here.

Catherine Edelman – *300 W. Superior St. 312-266-2350. www.edelmangallery.com.* This is one of the Midwest's leading galleries devoted exclusively to photography.

Marx-Saunders Gallery, Ltd. – *230 W. Superior St. 312-573-1400. www.marxsaunders.com.* Contemporary studio glass and sculpture fill the display space at Marx-Saunders.

Perimeter Gallery – *210 W. Superior St. 312-266-9473. www.perimetergallery.com.* Perimeter offers contemporary painting, sculpture, works on paper and master crafts.

Zolla/Lieberman Gallery – *325 W. Huron St. 312-944-1990. www.zollaliebermangallery.com.* The first gallery to come to River North, in 1975, showcases contemporary works by emerging and established artists.

Mart Smart

Chicago's wholesale furniture and design behemoth, the **Merchandise Mart** *(300 N. Wells St., River North; open Mon–Fri 9am–5pm; 312-527-7762; www.merchandisemart.com)* is second in size only to the Pentagon in Washington, DC. Most of the Mart is open only to card-carrying professionals, but the new **LuxeHome** boutiques welcome the public as well. Located on the first floor of the Mart and accessible by all entrances, LuxeHome includes 70,000 square feet and 25 kitchen and bath showrooms, featuring everything from fixtures to stonework. Check out the latest from Poggenpohl, Waterworks, de Giulio and others. Not in the market for a new Jacuzzi? Take a 90-minute tour of the wholesale merchandisers *(Mon & Fri 1pm; $10)*.

The blues rule in Chicago, and jazz is vice-president. There are plenty of venues to hear both, as well as other types of music—reggae, rock, house and hip-hop. Dance, drink, lounge to your heart's content, upscale or down. Oh, and there's a little comedy club here called **The Second City**, along with others in both stand-up and ensemble style.

Blues Clubs

Blue Chicago

736 N. Clark St.; 312-642-6261. Also at 536 N. Clark St.; 312-661-0100. www.bluechicago.com.

One cover charge gets you into both Blue Chicago clubs, just blocks apart from each other in River North. These newcomers are not your typical funky blues clubs, but they do offer good music. On Sunday afternoons, you can catch an all-ages blues concert at the Blue Chicago Store *(534 N. Clark St.; 312-661-1003).*

B.L.U.E.S.

2519 N. Halsted St., Lincoln Park. 773-528-1012. www.chicagobluesbar.com.

You feel like you can reach out and touch the performers in this tiny, smoky club. Quality musicians from across the city and a down-and-dirty atmosphere make this one of the most popular blues bars in town.

Buddy Guy's Legends

754 S. Wabash Ave., South Loop. 312-427-0333.

Blues headliners take the stage here around 10:30pm, but earlier audiences on Friday and Saturday are treated to free acoustic sets beginning at 6pm.

Singin' the Blues

Born in the dusty cotton fields of the Mississippi River delta, the musical genre called the blues evolved from African slave chants, work songs and spirituals into a uniquely American musical form. From the hollows, fields and churches of the rural South, migrants brought their music north to Chicago in the 1910s. As artists such as "Big Bill" Broonzy and "Papa" Charlie Jackson began to play together, a hybrid guitar-driven style based on urban themes emerged. In the 1940s musicians experimented with amplification, and by 1950 Chicago surfaced as the capital of the hard-driving electric blues, with Muddy Waters (McKinley Morganfield) as its king. Today, Chicago greats like Willie Dixon, Koko Taylor, Buddy Guy and others push the blues into the 21C.

House of Blues

329 N. Dearborn St., River North. 312-923-2000. www.hob.com.

Blues is big business here, along with classic rock, heavy metal and other genres. Try the Gospel Brunch with two seatings every Sunday *(9:30am & noon)* for a rockin' good time.

Kingston Mines

2548 N. Halsted St., Lincoln Park. 773-477-4646. www.kingstonmines.com.

Frequented by top-notch musicians and regular folk, this ramshackle blues club features live music until 4am (5am on Saturday). Every night, two top local bands take turns playing on the club's two stages. The place fills up quickly, and at 2am fans pour in from B.L.U.E.S. across the street, so arrive early to get a good seat.

Jazz Clubs

Andy's Jazz Club

11 E. Hubbard St., Magnificent Mile. 312-642-6805. www.andysjazzclub.com.

This one's a classic, and it offers jazz three times a day: at lunch, the cocktail hour and mid-evening. The food's not bad here, either.

Cotton Club

1710 S. Michigan Ave., South Loop. 312-341-9787.

Dress up and step out for an evening of cool jazz in the Cab Calloway Room or an "urban contemporary" DJ mix in the Gray Room.

Green Dolphin Street

2200 N. Ashland Ave., Bucktown. 773-395-0066.

This big, swanky dinner-and-dance spot features the best of both worlds. Expensive meals are served in the cool dining room, and diners are invited to stay and enjoy jazz (with lots of Latin) in the roomy club for a discounted cover charge. Or just come for the music; the joint starts jumpin' after 10pm.

Green Mill Jazz Club

4802 N. Broadway Ave., Uptown. 773-878-5552. www.greenmilljazz.com.

Al Capone's crew used to hang out in this charming jazz club; the interior looks much as it did back in the 1920s and 30s. Jazz acts perform seven nights a week, and the music plays until 4am (5am on Saturday). On Sunday evenings, thick-skinned poets read their works to the crowds who attend the infamous Uptown Poetry Slam competitions.

Joe Segal's Jazz Showcase

59 W. Grand Ave., Magnificent Mile. 312-670-2473. www.jazzshowcase.com.

"Where Jazz Lives in Chicago"—and how. Since 1947 Joe's been bringing jazz stars to his stage to the delight of Chicagoans. There's even a Sunday matinee where kids get in free *(4pm)*.

Pops for Champagne

2934 N. Sheffield St., Lakeview. 773-472-1000. www.popsforchampagne.com.

Elegant and sophisticated, but not snooty, Pops and the adjacent **Star Bar** *(773-472-7272)* make for a special night out. With over 100 champagnes and live jazz every night, a fireplace in winter and garden seating in summer, Pops sparkles for appetizers or dessert.

The Velvet Lounge

2128 S. Indiana Ave., Near South Side. 312-791-9050.

Blink and you'll miss this wonderful little bare-bones club, which offers excellent jazz Wednesday through Sunday nights.

Music and Dance Clubs

Double Door

1572 N. Milwaukee Ave., Wicker Park. 773-489-3160. www.doubledoor.com.

This is the premier live-music venue in the area. The owners book bands that are just breaking onto the national scene, and the small, V-shaped room is a great place to see future stars up-close.

Empty Bottle

1035 N. Western Ave., Wicker Park. 773-276-3600.

The Empty Bottle books an eclectic mix of experimental jazz, hot local rock acts and bands on the brink of national renown.

Excalibur

632 N. Dearborn St., River North. 312-266-1944.

Housed in the old Chicago Historical Society, the spacious Excalibur offers something for everyone: eating, dancing, and 12 separate bars ranging over three floors. Music options run from live to DJ, alternative to rock.

Jimmy's Woodlawn Tap

1172 E. 55th St., Hyde Park. 773-643-5516. This dimly lit tavern is the off-campus hangout for University of Chicago types. Jimmy's prices are low, the beer selection is good and the bartenders are friendly, so drop by for a cold one (and live jazz on Sunday nights).

Funky Buddha Lounge

728 W. Grand Ave., River West. 312-666-1695. www.funkybuddha.com.

This crowded, too-cool (and too-loud) dance lounge features DJ or live music—jazz, Latin, hip-hop and house—along with a retro-Zen eclectic scene.

Comedy Clubs

ImprovOlympic

3541 N. Clark St., Lakeview. 773-880-0199. www.improvolympic.com.

Primarily a club for aspiring comics, ImprovOlympic features an array of ensemble revues performed by teams of comedians-in-training. Shows run in two theaters seven days a week; some start as late as midnight.

The Second City

1616 N. Wells St., Old Town. 312-337-3992. www.secondcity.com.

What would we do without The Second City? Its satirical improv comedy has shaped the national sense of humor since the television show *Saturday Night Live* took to the air in 1975. The troupe was founded in Hyde Park on the city's South Side in 1955 as the Compass Players. Scores of comedians started here, including Alan Alda, Elaine May, Ed Asner, Ann Meara, Joan Rivers and a galaxy of *SNL* stars led by John Belushi, Dan Aykroyd, Gilda Radner and Mike Myers (now the voice of Shrek). The hilarity continues with regular no-holds-barred revues nightly on the Mainstage, the E.T.C. stage and Donny's Skybox.

Zanies

1548 N. Wells St., Old Town. 312-337-4027. www.chicago.zanies.com.

Oldest comedy club in the city, this well-worn venue has outlasted a dozen glitzier competitors. Name a stand-up comedian, and chances are he or she has performed here. The club usually features three comics a night: two up-and-coming performers and a well-known headliner.

Now for Something Completely Different

Tired of the same old bar scene? Try drinks and dessert at **Sugar** (*108 W. Kinzie St.; 312-822-9999*), where decadent confections, over-the-top candy-centric design and sweet after-dinner drinks come complete with a full bar.

Or maybe a wine bar would be fun tonight. Airy and fresh, **Bin 36** (*339 N. Dearborn St.; 312-755-9463; www.bin36.com*) offers unique wine-tasting flights at its sleek zinc bar.

Need a vacation from your vacation? Chicago has just the thing. Slip away for a couple of hours—or make a day of it—and indulge at one of the city's many pampering palaces.

Charles Ifergan

106 E. Oak St., Magnificent Mile. 312-642-4484. www.charlesifergan.com.

This establishment was among the first businesses on Oak Street, and today its friendly staff offers expert salon and spa services. Whether you get the works in a Day of Beauty or just go for a two-hour Executive Treatment, you'll emerge feeling like a whole new person.

Elizabeth Arden Red Door Salon and Spa

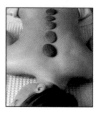

919 N. Michigan Ave. (enter on Walton St.), Magnificent Mile. 312-988-9191. www.reddoorspas.com.

The grand dame of all spas, and the classic choice of Chicago's most pampered, Elizabeth Arden's tony Red Door delivers skin care, massage, hydrotherapy and more with panache. Try an Elemental Balancing massage, in which aromatherapy oils are custom blended for you.

Kiva Day Spa

196 E. Pearson St., Magnificent Mile. 312-840-8120. www.premierspacollection.com.

Spa aficionados may recognize Kiva's parent company, the Premier Collection of Spas, with locations coast to coast. In Chicago, the southwestern surroundings are relaxing and welcoming. In addition to standard spa services, Kiva offers reflexology, cocoon therapies (choose from ayurvedic, marine, mother earth and more), and treatments for men.

Mario Tricoci

900 N. Michigan Ave., Magnificent Mile. 312-915-0960. www.tricoci.com.

Big, bold cousin of the **Red Door** (both are owned by Elizabeth Arden), Tricoci has locations all over Chicagoland. This huge facility offers everything from Spa-on-the-Go to the MT Signature Day of Beauty, among other packages. Or choose polishes, wraps, massages, hair, make-up and nail services à la carte.

Spa Space

161 N. Canal St., Near West Side. 312-466-9585. www.spaspace.com.

Situated downtown, this spa caters to busy professionals and offers a full line for men (Space Men, that is), including sports pedicures and back facials. With advance warning, meals or snacks can be ordered from restaurant Nine's spa menu, and the spa has its own juice bar.

Tiffani Kim Institute

310 W. Superior St., River North; 312-943-8777. Also in Park Hyatt Hotel, 800 N. Michigan Ave., Magnificent Mile; 312-239-4036. www.tiffanikiminstitute.com.

A smorgasbord of therapies, body treatments and relaxation awaits you at one of Tiffani Kim's two locations (the Park Hyatt spa includes a hair salon). Couples, best friends, and moms and daughters can book specialty services for two, such as facials and massages. And, the Institute even has a line of services for teens, both boys and girls. If you're in the market for a bridal gown, check out Tiffani Kim's stunning line of original designs.

Urban Oasis

939 W. North Ave. (garden level), Old Town; 312-640-0001. Also at 12 W. Maple St. (3rd floor), Gold Coast; 312-587-3500. www.urbanoasis.biz.

Massages are the order of the day here; from reiki and shiatsu, to hot-stone and deep-tissue, you'll find whatever your tired body needs. Try the salt glow, an exhilarating exfoliation treatment, followed by a 30-minute massage.

Urbanshe

1 E. Oak St. (2nd floor), Magnificent Mile. 312-988-9299. www.urbanshe.com.

Go for a facial, a wax (Brazilian is a specialty) or a massage, or book you and your gal pals for treatments and relaxation in the Shelounge. Primp for a wedding or a beach vacation. How about an eyebrow-arching party?

Thousand Waves Spa for Women

1212 W. Belmont, Lakeview. 773-549-0700. www.thousandwavesspa.com.

For women only, this serene, Japanese-style spa offers massages provided by women trained in a variety of techniques. Herbal wraps come in flavors from white pine bark to rosebud. All treatments begin in the three baths—dry sauna, eucalyptus steam and Jacuzzi sauna. If you only want to access the baths, no appointment is needed.

Nurture in Nature

Ensconced in beautiful Illinois farm country, **Heartland Spa** is a 90-mile jaunt from Chicago, but well worth the trip if you'd like to concentrate a few days on improving your fitness through exercise, diet and stress relief *(90 miles south of Chicago, off I-57 South; 1237 E. 1600 North Rd., Gilman, IL; 815-683-2182 or 800-545-4853; www.heartlandspa.com).* At this unpretentious oasis, you can take aerobic and strength classes, tai chi and yoga, and enjoy a full range of body treatments. Gourmet meals here are precisely nutritious and accommodations are simple but comfy.

Need a break from bustling downtown? A jaunt beyond the city limits reveals different worlds in any direction. Beaches and dunes lie south and east, history to the southwest, beautiful trees and great architecture to the west, and lovely gardens to the north. So take your pick!

Oak Park★★★

10mi west of Chicago via I-290 West to Harlem Ave. exit. Turn right on Harlem Ave. and proceed north. Visitor information: 708-524-7800 or 888-625-7275; www.visitoakpark.com. See map p 96.

What do the modern house, *For Whom the Bell Tolls* and Tarzan have in common? Oak Park, of course! Perhaps best known for its en-clave of homes designed by architect **Frank Lloyd Wright** *(see sidebar opposite),* Oak Park is also the birthplace of Ernest Hemingway and the one-time home of Edgar Rice Burroughs, creator of Tarzan.

Founded after the Great Chicago Fire in 1871 by a prosperous Puritan popula-tion, the little suburb grew rapidly. Today Oak Park is economically stable and socially progressive, accommodating various lifestyles with relative ease. Its shady, tree-lined streets, historic attractions, upscale boutiques and cozy restaurants make the suburb a must-see destination, especially for architec-ture buffs.

Touring Tip: Visiting Oak Park

If you arrive by car, the Lake Street parking garage *(between Kenilworth & Forest Aves.)* is most central to the attractions. To get there by public transportation, take the CTA Green or Blue Line, or take the Metra West commuter rail from the Metra station at W. Madison and Canal Sts. Exit all train lines at Oak Park Ave. or Harlem Ave. *(schedule and fares: 312-836-7000. www.metrarail.com).* You can catch the Oak Park Shuttle at train stations and various attractions around town *(10am–5:30pm daily, except major holidays; for information, call 708-615-1830).*

The **Oak Park Visitors Center** *(158 N. Forest Ave.; 708-524-7800; www.visit oakpark.com; open year-round daily 10am–5pm; closed Jan 1, Thanksgiving Day & Dec 25)* is a good place to pick up maps and guides, buy attraction tickets, and rent a guided audio tour for your walk around the neighborhood *($9).* Wright's Home and Studio *(opposite)* offers historic-district walking tours daily by audio *(10am–3:30pm; $9)* and by docent *(weekends only, Mar–Nov 11am–4pm, Dec–Feb noon, 1pm & 2pm; $9).* Purchase tickets and begin tours at the **Gingko Tree Bookshop** *(951 Chicago Ave.; 708-848-1606; open year-round daily 10am–5pm; closed major holidays).*

The Wright Stuff

Frank Lloyd Wright Home and Studio★★

951 Chicago Ave. 708-848-1976. www.wrightplus.org. Visit by 45min guided tour only, year-round Mon–Fri 11am, 1pm & 3pm; weekends 11am–3pm. Closed Jan 1, Thanksgiving Day & Dec 25. $9.

Wright first built this house in 1889 and continued to remodel and add to it over time; his alterations reveal his architectural growth. Restored to its 1909 appearance, when Wright last lived there, the original structure features the horizontal bands of windows and low profile of the Prairie style. Notice the cozy inglenook in the living room and the signature furnishings, built-in and freestanding, all designed by Wright.

Unity Temple★★

875 W. Lake St. 708-383-8873. www.unitytemple-utrf.org. Open Dec–Feb daily 1pm–4pm. Rest of the year Mon–Fri 10:30am–4:30pm, weekends 1pm–4pm. Guided tours weekends 1pm, 2pm & 3pm. Closed Jan 1, Thanksgiving Day & Dec 25.

Wright called this Unitarian temple "my jewel," and it's easy to see why. This, the last of his major public buildings still standing, is currently undergoing a thorough restoration scheduled for completion on the building's 100th anniversary in 2008.

Forest Avenue★

Walk south from Wright's home and studio to see a wonderful cross-section of his residential work (pick up information at the visitor center). Begin by wandering west on Chicago Avenue. Numbers 1019, 1027 and 1031 are "bootleg" homes that the 25-year-old architect designed in violation of his exclusive contract with Adler & Sullivan in 1892–93. The 1902 **Frank W. Thomas House**★ at no. 210 is considered Wright's first true Prairie-style house; it abandons all the fuss of Victorian design that you see in the row houses just south.

Frank Lloyd Wright

Frank Lloyd Wright's best-known works revolutionized residential building design. Born in Wisconsin in 1867, Wright came early under the influence of renowned architect Louis Sullivan, apprenticing in Sullivan's studio until striking out on his own at age 25. Living and working in Oak Park, he developed his distinctive Prairie style, its strong horizontal lines and overhanging eaves inspired by the flat midwestern landscape. Inside, Wright flowed rooms one into another and he designed furniture to complement his organic designs. In a scandal that effectively ended his practice in socially conservative Oak Park, Wright left his wife and six children in 1909. Wright remained in the limelight until his death in 1959 at age 91. His total number of designs exceeds 1,100, nearly half of which were actually built.

The Rest of Oak Park's Best

"Pleasant Home"★

217 S. Home Ave. 708-383-2654. www.oprf.com/phf. Visit by 1-hour guided tour only, Mar–Nov 12:30pm, 1:30pm & 2:30pm. Rest of the year Thu–Sun 12:30pm & 1:30pm. Closed major holidays. $5.

Here's a Prairie-style home designed by another architect, George Washington Maher (1864–1926), whose work can be seen throughout the suburbs of Chicago. He designed the 30-room "Pleasant Home" (aka Farson-Mills House) in 1897 for banker John Farson.

Ernest Hemingway Birthplace

339 N. Oak Park Ave. 708-848-2222. www.hemingway.org. Visit by guided tour only, year-round Sun–Fri 1pm–5pm, Sat 10am–5pm. $7.

This restored Victorian home built in 1890 re-creates the comfortable family upbringing of celebrated author Ernest Hemingway (1899–1961). A visit here also provides a glimpse of Oak Park's social order in the early 20C and the impact that the community had on the author's early development. Two blocks south, the **Hemingway Museum** *(200 N. Oak Park Ave.; same hours & contact information as Birthplace; $7)* focuses on the first 20 years of the writer's life.

Brookfield Zoo★★ – *8400 W. 31st St. See Musts for Kids.*

Map:

- ★★ Frank Lloyd Wright Home & Studio
- Chicago Ave.
- River Forest
- Oak St.
- Quick Ave.
- Pl. Brae
- Holly Ct.
- Cummings Square
- Clinton
- Bonnie
- Central Ave.
- Circle Ave.
- Franklin St.
- Forest
- Dixon St.
- Park
- 1031 1027 1019
- Moore House
- Hills-DeCaro House
- Heurtley House
- Elizabeth Ct.
- Gale House
- Thomas House ★
- Ontario
- Austin Gardens Park
- ★★★ OAK PARK
- Oak Park Visitors Center
- Harlem
- Lake St.
- HARLEM/LAKE
- ★★ Unity Temple
- South Blvd.
- ★ "Pleasant Home"
- Pleasant St.
- Mills Park
- Randolph St.
- Maple Marion
- Grove Ave.
- Park Ave.
- Ernest Hemingway Birthplace
- Erie St.
- Hemingway Museum
- Oak
- Scoville Park
- North
- Chicago Ave.
- Superior St.
- Oak Park-River Forest High School
- Lake Blvd.
- Scoville
- Elmwood
- Ridgeland
- Kenilworth
- Euclid
- Linden
- Oak Park
- East St.
- Ridgeland Common
- RIDGELAND
- Pleasant St.
- 0   1/5 mi
- 0   400 m

Hotels
- 🏨 The Carleton of Oak Park
- 🏨 The Write Inn

Restaurants
- ❶ Avenue Ale House
- ❷ Café le Coq

North Shore★★

31mi from downtown Chicago to Lake Forest. Follow Lake Shore Dr. /Sheridan Rd. north.

Chicago's northern suburbs collectively conjure up a vision of elegant living called the North Shore. The lovely—and unusual—geography of ravines, bluffs, beaches and woodlands, and the area's architecture and history combine to make a drive up the shore an enjoyable one-day excursion. Take your time and stop for lunch, take a peek around a village center, or a enjoy one of the many beaches along the way. (During summer, some townships charge nonresidents for beach or park admission.)

Getting To Know the North Shore

Baha'i House of Worship★★

100 Linden Ave., Wilmette. 847-853-2300. www.us.bahai.org/how. Open year-round daily 7am–6:30pm; visitor center open year-round daily 10am–5pm. Guided tours Sun 1:45pm.

The lacy, opalescent dome of the Baha'i temple will startle you as you cross from Evanston to Wilmette on Sheridan Road. The mammoth, nine-sided structure, rising 191 feet, cuts an exotic profile against the low suburban skyline. This is the North American seat of the Baha'i faith, whose members follow the teachings of the 19C Persian prophet Baha'u'llah, believing in the "oneness" of religion and of humankind. Why is the only North American temple located here? The religion was introduced at the 1893 World's Columbian Exposition held in Chicago. Construction of the temple, which began in 1909, took nearly 50 years to complete.

North Shore Rest Stops

Downtown Evanston and Central Street a little farther north both teem with restaurants and shops. In Wilmette, try **Convito Italiano** *(1515 Sheridan Rd., in Plaza del Lago; 847-251-0123; www.convitoitaliano.com)* for a delightful trattoria lunch or dinner, or the makings of a gourmet picnic from its market. Tiny **Ravinia Bistro** *(581 Roger Williams Ave., Highland Park; 847-432-1033)* serves French country fare and delectable pastries. Along Sheridan Road in Highwood, you'll find a gaggle of notable French and Italian restaurants. When you reach Lake Forest, stop by **Market Square**★ *(700 N. Western Ave.)*, a village shopping and dining center since the early 1900s.

Chicago Botanic Garden★★

1000 Lake Cook Rd., Glencoe. 25mi north of Chicago via I-90/94 West to I-94 and US-41. Exit at Lake Cook Rd. and go east .5mi. 847-835-5440. www.chicago-botanic.org. Open year-round daily 8am–dusk. Closed Dec 25. Parking $10/car.

With 26 garden areas, more than a million individual plants of 7,000 different varieties and a host of bird life, the 385-acre preserve makes a lovely stop at any time of year. The heart of the garden occupies the largest of nine islands in a 60-acre artificial lagoon.

Begin at the **Gateway Visitor Center**, and consider a tram tour *(late Apr–Oct daily 10am–3:30pm; $5)* for a narrated overview. Highlights include the formal **Rose Garden**★, the six "rooms" of the **English Walled Garden**★, the tactile and fragrant **Sensory Garden**, and the **Japanese Garden**★, called Sansho-En ("the garden of three islands"). In summer, kids will enjoy the **Model Railroad Garden**, 7,500 square feet of miniature American landscapes crisscrossed by 15 model train lines *(open daily 10am–5pm; $3)*. You can have a sit-down lunch or a snack here, too, in the **Garden Café**, the outdoor **Grille**, or the **Rose Terrace Café**.

Morton Arboretum★

4100 Rte. 53, Lisle. 25mi west of downtown via I-290 West to I-88 tollway West; exit on Rte. 53 and go north. 630-968-0074. www.mortonarb.org. Open Apr–Oct daily 7am–7pm. Rest of the year daily 7am–5pm. $5.

Joy Morton used the fortune he made at the helm of Morton Salt Company to establish this arboretum on 400 acres in 1922. Today sprawling over 1,700 acres, the outdoor museum is both a serious scientific laboratory of woody plants from around the world and a lovely place to spend the day. You'll find oaks, elms, lindens, sugar maples and 3,300 other tree and plant types organized into family groups, landscape groups, geographic groups and habitat groups. Whether you choose to hike the 14 miles of trails, drive the 9-mile circuit or spend the day exploring the new 36,000-square-foot **visitor center** and surrounding gardens, you're in for a treat. A new Children's Garden and a one-acre hedge Maze Garden are due for completion in 2005.

Touring Tip

During good weather, enjoy the full sweep of the arboretum on the **Acorn Express**, a narrated, one-hour open-air tram tour *(departs from the visitor center year-round; 630-968-0074; $4)*.

Illinois & Michigan Canal National Heritage Corridor★

Southwest of Chicago via I-55 South to Rtes. 45 & 171. Visitor information: Heritage Corridor Convention and Visitors Bureau, 800-925-2262 or www.heritagecorridorcvb. com; and the Canal Corridor Association, 815-588-1100 or www.canalcor.org.

Running 96 miles from Bridgeport to LaSalle/Peru, the Illinois & Michigan (I&M) Canal first linked the Great Lakes to the Mississippi in 1848 and helped Chicago build its reputation as an industrial powerhouse. Until 1882 when steamboats took over, mules pulled barges laden with lumber, stone and grains through 15 locks that equalized the 160-foot difference in water level between the canal in Chicago and the Illinois River. By 1914, the new Sanitary and Ship Canal replaced the northern section, and in 1933 the Illinois River was made navigable in the southern reaches.

> **Best Ways to Experience the National Heritage Corridor**
>
> The scenic 61-mile **I&M Canal State Trail**★ runs along the old towpath from Rockdale to LaSalle *(access at Channahon, Exit 248 from I-55)* and provides a historic route you can hike, bike or snowmobile. At LaSalle, where the canal and Heritage Corridor end, you'll find **Lock no. 14**★, the only lock that is completely restored *(Canal Rd., off Rte. 351).*

Now long obsolete, the canal is preserved in a **National Heritage Corridor** and a series of parks, trails and preserves. The waterway passes through suburbs and industrial areas, as well as the historic canal towns of **Lemont**, **Lockport**★, **Joliet**★, **Morris**, **Seneca**, **Marseilles**, **Ottawa**★, **Utica** and **LaSalle**, some more ravaged than burnished by time.

Lockport★

15mi southwest of Chicago via I-55 South to LaGrange Rd./Rte. 45 (Exit 279A).

As the location of Lock no. 1 and the old Canal Commission headquarters, Lockport once bustled with the comings and goings of barges, canallers, merchants, wagons and mules. Old grain warehouses—the Gaylord and the Norton buildings—bookend the historic district, which encompasses the blocks between the canal and 7th, Washington and 11th streets. Restored to its 1860s appearance, the **Gaylord Building**★ *(200 W. 8th St.; 815-588-1100; www.canalcor.org/gaylord; open year-round Tue–Sat 10am–6pm, Sun noon–6pm)* features an information desk and exhibits that explore the history of the canal and its impact on Illinois. To the south, the 1850 **Norton Building** now houses the **Lockport Gallery**, which exhibits the work of past and present Illinois artists *(201 W. 10th St.; 815-838-7400; www.museum.stat.il.us/ismsites/ lockport; open year-round Tue–Sat 10am–5pm, Sun noon–5pm; closed major holidays).*

In between the Gaylord and Norton buildings, the **Pioneer Settlement**★ *(815-838-5080; open May–Oct 1 daily 1pm–4:30pm)* of 19C buildings spreads for a block along the canal's edge. The **I&M Canal Museum** is located in the original Canal Commission head-quarters *(803 South State St.; 815-838-5080; visit by guided tour only, year-round daily 1pm–4:30pm)*.

Walk the 2.5-mile **Gaylord Donnelley Canal Trail**★ for a look at the massive limestone walls of Lock no. 1. West of the canal extends the lovely, 269-acre **Lockport Prairie Nature Preserve**★ *(Rte. 53 & Division St.; 815-727-8700; www.fpdwc.org/lockport.cfm; open Apr–Oct daily 8am–8pm; rest of the year daily 8am–5pm).*

Fine Dining on the Prairie

One of the region's finest restaurants occupies a restored 1895 building in Lockport's historic district. **Tallgrass** *(1006 S. State St.; 815-838-5566)* offers contemporary French cuisine in prix-fixe menus of three, four or five courses. For lunch, or a less pricey dinner, choose **Public Landing** *(815-838-6500)*, located in the Gaylord Building. Farther down the pike, enjoy lunch or dinner in the rustic supper-club atmosphere at **Starved Rock Lodge** *(Rtes. 178 & 71; 800-868-7625; www.starvedrocklodge.com).*

Ottawa★

79mi southwest of Chicago via I-55 South to Rte. 23 (Exit 90).

This town was built on glass. Silica sand from its famous quarries was shipped to and fro on the canal, and by 1900, the city was a leading glass producer. In **Washington Park**, senatorial candidates Abraham Lincoln and Stephen A. Douglas held the first of their famous 1858 debates. Douglas was a frequent guest at the 1856 **Reddick Mansion**★, adjacent to the park *(100 W. Lafayette St.; 815-434-2737; www.experienceottawa.com; open year round Mon–Fri 9am–5pm, Sat 9am–4pm, Sun 10am–2pm).*

Barging

Before railroads, canals transported people west and products east. Along with the Erie Canal, the I&M provided an inland link from New York to New Orleans. Up and down the I&M, young canal boys led mules along towpaths pulling 100-foot barges, each loaded with 100 tons of cargo. Today, on the Sanitary and Ship Canal, which runs parallel to the old I&M, one barge can carry 15 times the freight, and tugboats now replace the boys and their mules.

To watch a modern lock in operation, stop in Utica at the **Illinois Waterway Visitor Center**★ *(950 N. 27th Rd.; 815-667-4054; open year round daily 9am–5pm).*

Indiana Dunes National Lakeshore★

40mi south of Chicago via I-94/I-90 to I-90; exit at US-20/US-12. Follow US-12 to the lakeshore sites. Visitor information: 219-926-7561, ext. 225; www.nps.gov/indu.

Looking for a brawnier beach than Chicago offers? Then head south to this 25-mile sliver of pristine land wedged around the heavy industry of northern Indiana. It's about a 40-mile drive, but don't let the intervening smokestacks deter you; the 15,000 acres of windswept beaches, dunes, marshes and forests of this National Lakeshore are worth the trip. Though brawny they may look, these ancient glacial dunes form a fragile eco-system at the mercy of prevailing winds, pounding waves and human encroachment. The titanic effort to preserve them began in 1911 and continues to this day.

Bailly Homestead and Chellberg Farm and Trail★

On Mineral Springs Rd., 6mi east of Inland Marsh. Open year round 8am–dusk.

Though access to these historic buildings is limited to a few occasions a year, a trek around the 2-mile trail here reveals a glimpse of early settlement as well as the natural wonders of the dunes.

Mount Baldy★

One of the largest (123 feet) dunes in the park, Mt. Baldy is constantly being pushed inland by the winds, at a rate of 4 to 5 feet a year. The walk up and around the dune to the beach is short *(.5mi)* and very steep—be careful! And no, that massive tower you see is not a nuclear plant, but a garden-variety power-plant cooling tower.

West Beach Area★

Turn left on County Line Rd., shortly after entering the park. Open May–Sept daily 9am–9pm. Rest of the year daily 8am–dusk. $6/car mid-May–end of Sept. Pets prohibited. Beware of dangerous undertow when swimming.

Known primarily for its popular West Beach, this large section of the park also includes Long Lake and 3.5 miles of hiking trails. A walk along the **Dune Succession Trail**★ offers a look at the park's surprising biological diversity, encompassing 1,400 plant species, and a number of excellent **viewpoints**★.

Indiana Dunes State Park

1600 North 25 East, Chesterton, Indiana. 219-926-1952. www.state.in.us/dnr/parklake/parks/indianadunes.html. Open year-round daily 7am–11pm. $8/vehicle ($4/vehicle for Indiana residents). Ensconced within the greater national lakeshore, the state park offers 3 miles of beachfront and 16.5 miles of trails. Amenities here include a bathhouse/pavilion, picnic areas and a visitor center.

The venues listed below were selected for their ambience, location and/or value for money. Rates indicate the average cost of an appetizer, an entrée and a dessert for one person (not including tax, gratuity or beverages). Most restaurants are open daily (except where noted) and accept major credit cards. Call for information regarding reservations, dress code and opening hours. For a list of restaurants organized by theme (Special Occasion, Easy on the Budget, etc.), see p 113.

$$$$	Over $50	**$$**	$15–$30
$$$	$30–$50	**$**	Under $15

Luxury

Ambria
$$$$ French

2300 Lincoln Park West, Lincoln Park. Dinner only. Closed Sun. 773-472-5959. www.leye.com.

This elegant restaurant, decorated with dark woods, ultrasuede banquettes and miniature lamps on each table, consistently ranks at the top of both critics' and diners' lists. Candlelight, a fireplace in winter and classical music in the background set the mood for romance. Chef Gabino Sotelino (who also owns and manages the restaurant) prepares scrumptious, exquisitely presented French cuisine such as terrine of foie gras, sautéed veal tenderloin, and smoked wild sea bass and scallops. To complement the chef's creations, Ambria boasts an extensive, award-winning wine list. Across the lobby, **Un Grand Café** *(773-348-8886)* serves up bistro atmosphere and classic French fare.

Arun's
$$$$ Thai

4156 N. Kedzie Ave., Wrigleyville. Dinner only. Closed Mon. 773-539-1909. www.arunsthai.com.

Reputedly among the best Thai restaurants in the country, Arun's made a bold move some years back: they dropped their standard menu in favor of a 12-course prix-fixe menu *($75)*. And it seems to be a hit. Against a backdrop of mahogany, Thai silk, wall murals and Thai craftwork, diners here can sample a delightful array of delicacies and flavors selected and blended with exquisite attention to detail. Whereas the six appetizer courses are served one by one, the entrées are served family style. Choices can range from snapper in red tamarind sauce to "golden baskets," a house specialty of shrimp-and-chicken-filled pastries. The meal ends with Arun's palate-cleansing lemongrass elixir.

Charlie Trotter's $$$$ New American

816 W. Armitage Ave., Lincoln Park. Dinner only. Closed Sun & Mon. Jackets required.
773-248-6228. www.charlietrotters.com.

Tables at the restaurant run by culinary genius
Charlie Trotter get booked 4 to 12 weeks in advance. The draw? One-of-a-kind dishes prepared
with naturally raised meats, organic produce and
vegetable-based sauces. Choose from two daily
eight-course prix-fixe menus, the grand dégusta-
tion menu *($135)* and the lighter vegetable menu
($115). For a special treat, reserve the sole kitchen
table, where cooking becomes performance.

Everest $$$$ French

440 S. LaSalle St., in One Financial Place, Loop. 312-663-8920. Dinner only.
Closed Sun & Mon. www.everestrestaurant.com.

Named for its lofty perch on the 40th floor of the Chicago Stock Exchange,
Everest commands a sweeping view of the city. Award-winning chef Jean Joho
(also of Brasserie Jo; *p 105*) crafts the finest seasonal ingredients into mouth-
watering creations, adding accents from his native Alsace. Order à la carte to
sample some of Joho's signature dishes—foie gras terrine, apple and Alsace
Tokay gelée; roasted Maine lobster in Alsatian Gewurztraminer butter and
ginger—or be adventurous and try the tasting menu *(seven courses for $89)*.

Pluton $$$$ American Regional

873 N. Orleans St., River North. Dinner only. Closed Sun & Mon. 312-266-1440.
www.plutonrestaurant.com.

Named for chef Jacky Pluton, this restaurant exudes an unpretentious air of
formality with its understated décor. Select among three prix-fixe tasting
menus: create your own 5-course meal *($99)*, or let the chef surprise you with
seasonal samplings of 7 *($119)* or 10 *($129)* courses. Choices on the 5-course
menu include the likes of miro bass with foie gras ravioli, and white-chocolate
coconut pyramid with fruit minestrone. To accompany your meal, you can
choose from among the restaurant's list of more than 500 labels.

Spiaggia

$$$$ Italian

980 N. Michigan Ave., 2nd floor of One Magnificent Mile Building, Magnificent Mile. Dinner only. Jackets required. 312-280-2750. www.levyrestaurants.com.

Overlooking Oak Street Beach and Lake Michigan through its floor-to-ceiling windows on the north end of Michigan Avenue, Chicago's toniest Italian restaurant offers a soaring array of dishes that are well-grounded in regional Italian cuisine. Pastas are handmade; meat and fish are wood-roasted—try the signature Colorado lamb chop with polenta and Brussels sprouts. Next door, dressed-down **Café Spiaggia** *(lunch Mon–Sat, dinner nightly, brunch Sun)* serves tasty pizzas and pastas at more palatable prices.

Tru

$$$$ New American

676 N. St. Clair St., Magnificent Mile. Dinner only. Closed Sun. Reservations required. 312-202-0001. www.trurestaurant.com.

At once lush and spare, the dining room at Tru sets the stage for the epicurean theater to follow. Original Warhols and other artworks add color to the room, and the tables are serenely minimalist. After you choose from four prix-fixe menus, the fun begins. Award win-ning chefs Rick Tramonto and Gale Gand (of Food Network fame) send out course after course, each more exquisite than the last in both food and presentation. These are not large courses, mind you, but jewel-like creations to tease the palate. Dinner takes about three hours when served this way, but it's a lovely, sensual experience.

Moderate

Bistro 110

$$$ French

110 E. Pearson St., Magnificent Mile. 312-266-3110. www.bistro110restaurant.com.
The roasted garlic bulb that accompanies your baguette at this bright, bustling French bistro sets the tone for the wood-oven-roasted meats and fish served

here—all redolent with garlic. Good basic *steak au poivre* and *steaks frites* are sure to satisfy, as are bistro favorites like cassoulet Toulousian and Robu-chon lamb shank, slow-roasted in its own juices. This is a great place for a lunch break while shop-ping on Mag Mile.

Blackbird

$$$ New American

619 W. Randolph St., Near West Side. Closed Sun. 312-715-0708. www.blackbirdrestaurant.com.
In contrast to its stark white exterior and minimalist décor, this tiny Market District hot spot serves dishes that are a feast for the eyes, prepared in a style that acclaimed chef Paul Kahan describes as "seasonal American with French countryside influ-ences." The name Blackbird comes from French slang for a plump Merlot grape. Try the signature wood-grilled California sturgeon, or perhaps a stuffed breast of bob-white quail with medjool dates, lobster mushrooms and white-corn grits. You never know what you might find; the menu and wine list both change frequently.

Brasserie Jo$$$ French

59 W. Hubbard St., River North. Dinner only. 312-595-0800. www.brasseriejo.com.

Chef Jean Joho (also of the dressier Everest; *see p 103*) works magic with the country fare of Alsace, offering among other hearty dishes a marvelous sausage choucroute, a flaky onion tart, a lobster bouillabaisse, and the restaurant's "Famous Shrimp Bag" (shrimp and vegetables bathed in a light cream sauce and steamed in a phyllo bag). The largely Alsatian wine list, good beer and authentic Parisian brasserie atmosphere complete this delightful dining experience. Bring the kids; they get some surprises along with their own menu.

Green Zebra$$$ Vegetarian

1460 W. Chicago Ave., River West. Dinner only. Closed Mon. 312-243-7100. www.greenzebrachicago.com.

Chicago may be prized for its beef, but you couldn't tell it by Green Zebra, which has been packing in crowds of vegetarians since it opened in spring 2004. Named for a variety of heirloom tomato, this hot spot pulses with a hip vibe evident in its buzzing dining room and techno-modern décor. Chef Shawn McClain displays his culinary artistry using the freshest

offerings of the season in selections like silky avocado panna cotta with tomato gelée, crème fraiche and sweet corn chips; and cave-aged-gruyère soufflé with endive and heirloom apples. Save room for the white-chocolate dreamsicle, with vanilla-bean ice cream, orange granité and ginger soda.

Harry Caray's$$$ American

33 W. Kinzie Ave., River North. 312-828-0966. www.harrycarays.com.

Cub fans will revel in the atmosphere here, which is chock-full of baseball memorabilia and items relating to the Hall of Fame career of late baseball announcer Harry Caray. House specialty chicken Vesuvio (chicken sautéed with garlic, then baked with crispy potatoes and served with peas and a white-wine reduction) and 23-ounce Prime Porterhouse steaks top the menu. The 60-foot-long bar makes a great gathering place. Prices range widely so there's something for everyone.

The Pump Room$$$ New American

In the Omni Ambassador East Hotel, 1301 N. State Pkwy., Gold Coast. 312-266-0360. www.pumproom.com.

In its heyday during the 1940s, this restaurant was *the* place for Chicago's swell set and visiting Hollywood stars to see and be seen. They undoubtedly came for the outrageous service—dishes were delivered on flaming swords, and guests' dogs could dine in the adjacent Pup Room. While it's no longer the center of Chicago society, the Pump Room remains a charming, elegant restaurant with excellent food. Rumors are it's becoming fashionable again.

Rhapsody
$$$ New American

65 E. Adams St., Loop. Closed Sun. 312-786-9911. www.rhapsodychicago.com.

Much of the charm of this elegant urban dining spot derives from its location in Symphony Center at the heart of Chicago's Loop, which is framed beautifully in the restaurant's glass window-walls. Eclectic and inventive dishes (coq au vin blanc, Nantucket Bay scallops glazed with orange reduction) and desserts worthy of an encore draw on flavors from around the world. Wrap up your meal with the aptly named Chocolate Symphony, a sampling of bittersweet chocolate crème caramel, molten chocolate brownie and white praline hot chocolate. Reserve early on performance nights. *No gym shoes, blue jeans or shorts.*

Russian Tea Time
$$$ Russian

77 E. Adams St., Loop. 312-360-0000. www.russianteatime.com.

Distinguished by red-velvet furnishings, this elegant (if over the top) tea room located one block from the Art Institute buzzes with the polite chatter of classical-music lovers when the symphony performs. Fine caviar and champagne are de rigueur in the evening as is tea in the afternoon. The restaurant also offers a complete menu for lunch and dinner featuring Russian, Uzbek, Ukrainian and Baltic delicacies. Like Rhapsody, this is another restaurant that's popular with the symphony crowd, so reserve early.

Saloon Steakhouse
$$$ American

200 E. Chestnut St., Magnificent Mile. No lunch weekends. 312-280-5454. www.saloonsteakhouse.com.

There are plenty of good steakhouses in Chicago. It's the atmosphere at the Saloon that sets it apart—more a neighborhood tavern than a swanky steakhouse. The room is small, but comfortable, and the steaks, vegetables and potato sides keep 'em coming back for more. Among its other fine cuts, The Saloon serves Wagyu beef, which is American-raised Kobe-style beef. Added benefits: the service is friendly and the wine list is long.

Tizi Melloul
$$$ Moroccan

535 N. Wells St., River North. Dinner only. 312-670-4338. www.tizimelloul.com.

Wonderful contemporary Moroccan and Mediterranean cuisine is served here amid billowing curtains and pillows in rich reds and golds. Every inch the casbah, Tizi Melloul is a lot of fun. Start with a refreshing Rockin' Moroccan cocktail (vodka, lime juice, fresh mint, soda water and a splash of Sprite), then dive into the fire-roasted mussels. The tagine (lamb and dates stewed in a special clay pot and served over toasted orzo) makes a particularly good entrée. After dinner, lounge in the bar with a nightcap and a hookah. Come Sunday nights to catch the belly dancing.

Topolobampo
$$$ Mexican Regional

445 N. Clark St., River North. Closed Sun & Mon. 312-661-1434. www.fronterakitchens.com.

Chef Rick Bayless has given his sophisticated cuisine a nationwide reputation by the skillful blending of traditional Mexican flavors from Yucatan to Oaxaca. The chef's way with chilies and mole is particularly notable, and fish dishes excel. The menu changes every two weeks, but *puerco en manchamanteles* (Maple Creek Farm pork loin in red-chile sauce with plantains, pineapple and

homemade chorizo) and *pescado en mole Amarillo* (pan-seared day-boat catch in Oaxacan yellow mole with smoked Prince Edward Island mussels and red-chile rice) are typical of the chef's culinary artistry. You'll find the same quality—at less cost—at the more casual **Frontera Grill**, which shares space with Topolobampo.

Inexpensive

Andies
$$ Mediterranean

5253 N. Clark St., Andersonville. 773-784-8616. www.andiesres.com.

It may be off the beaten path, but if you're up this way at lunch or dinnertime, give Andies a try. A nice fireplace warms up the whitewashed room, which is clean and inviting. The menu blends Mediterranean and Middle Eastern flavors into an impressive montage of dishes at very reasonable prices. Ingredients are always fresh, and the service is friendly. Andies also features a kids' menu. You'll find another location a little farther south at 1467 West Montrose Avenue *(773-348-0654)*.

The Berghoff
$$ German

17 W. Adams St., Loop. Closed Sun. 312-427-3170. www.berghoff.com.

Founded in 1898 by brewer Herman Berghoff, this spacious German restaurant is one of the oldest operating taverns in the city. The sauerbraten, schnitzel and creamed spinach draw huge lunchtime crowds. The adjacent stand-up bar (no seating), best known for its bratwurst and its potato salad, caters to diners on the run. But its authentic 19C atmosphere and carved wood may make you want to linger.

Cafe Ba-Ba-Reeba!
$$ Spanish

2024 N. Halsted St., Lincoln Park. 773-935-5000. www.leye.com.

Though other tapas bars have cropped up since, this was Chicago's original. Seven seating areas decked in bright Mediterranean colors accommodate 360 diners. Ambience and food still sizzle, and the crowds come to enjoy hot and cold tapas ("little dishes" ordered in quantity and shared), paella, and a nice selection of Spanish wines.

Club Lucky $$ Italian

1824 W. Wabansia Ave., Bucktown. 773-227-2300. www.club-lucky.com.

In a neighborhood where eateries come and go, Club Lucky has endured. Generous portions of homestyle Italian cooking—rigatoni with veal meatballs, eggplant parmigiana, shrimp scampi, chicken oreganato—great martinis and a funky 1940s supper-club atmosphere team up to make this lounge/restaurant a long-lived hit.

Erwin $$ American

2925 N. Halsted St., Lakeview. Dinner only (brunch Sun). Closed Mon. 773-528-7200. www.erwincafe.com.

Seasonal specialties with Midwestern flavor grace Erwin's simple but robust menu. Creative vegetable and fruit preparations and savory sauces embellish basics like calves liver, pan-roasted Great Lakes whitefish, wood-grilled pork chops, and even hamburger—served with fries, horseradish slaw and homemade pickles. The smallish room is casual yet chic and comfortable, with the feel of a friend's dining room.

Gino's East $$ Pizza

633 N. Wells St., River North. 312-988-2400. www.featuredfoods.com.

Chicago's favorite deep-dish pizzeria, renowned for its two-inch-thick pies and its graffiti-splattered wooden booths, which have been moved to a new location in the space once occupied by Planet Hollywood. Call ahead and order your pizza, or be prepared to wait at least 30 minutes for your pie to cook.

Heaven on Seven $$ Cajun

111 N. Wabash Ave., 7th floor of Garland Building, Loop. Breakfast & lunch Mon–Sat. Dinner third Fri of month (reservations required). Closed Sun. 312-263-6443. www.heavenonseven.com.

Creole shrimp, crab cakes, po-boy sandwiches and gumbo are just a few of the New Orleans-style dishes served in this small but bustling lunchroom. Most entrées are served plenty spicy, but connoisseurs of Cajun heat use the bottles of Louisiana hot sauce on the tables to season their food. For a sweet ending, try a healthy serving of cinnamon-spiked bread pudding. A slicker version of the original, **Heaven on Seven on Rush** *(600 N. Michigan Ave., 2nd floor; 312-280-7774)* serves lunch and dinner daily. Or try the Wrigleyville location at 3478 N. Clark Street *(773-477-7818).*

Pasteur
$$ Vietnamese

5525 N. Broadway, Uptown. 773-878-1061.

Located just blocks north of Chicago's enclave of Viet-
namese restaurants on Argyle Street, this gem distin-
guishes itself in presentation, décor and cuisine. Sur-
rounded by palm trees, diners enjoy a range of carefully
prepared regional specialties from Saigon to Hanoi in the
cool and inviting dining room. The clay-pot chicken gets
raves, and the whole red snapper is a house specialty.

Ann Sather
$ Swedish-American

929 W. Belmont Ave., Lakeview. Breakfast & lunch daily, dinner Wed–Sun.
773-348-2378. www.annsather.com.

A welcoming atmosphere and home cooking with a Swedish flair have made
this a favorite among Chicagoans since 1945. Breakfast is a specialty—think
Swedish pancakes with lingonberries or Swedish meatballs. And be sure to try
the homemade cinnamon rolls. Reasonably priced dinner entrées (baked
chicken, Tom turkey, Lake Superior whitefish) come with two sides and des-
sert. Belmont Avenue is the flagship, but Ann Sather now has locations in
Andersonville, Wicker Park and Lincoln Park.

Chicago Pizza and Oven Grinder
$ Italian

2121 N. Clark St., Lincoln Park. Dinner only Mon–Fri, lunch weekends. 773-248-2570.
www.chicagopizzaandovengrinder.com.

Located across the street from the site of the
St. Valentine's Day Massacre, this nook in the base-
ment of a Victorian brownstone serves unusual
topsy-turvy pizzas that resemble potpies. Abundant
salads can be shared and the grinders (the local
term for submarine sandwiches) are generous.
Good food and the laid-back atmosphere make this
place popular and the waits sometimes long.

Ed Debevic's
$ American

640 N. Wells St., River North. 312-664-1707. www.featuredfoods.com.

"Good food, fresh service": that's the mantra of this Chicago institution, known
for its sassy waitstaff who talk back and randomly jump up on the counter to
sing. But kids and tourists seem to love it, and the diner fare—chili, burgers,
hot dogs, meatloaf, ribs, milkshakes and thick malts—isn't bad either.

Gold Coast Dogs
$ American

159 N. Wabash Ave., Loop. 312-917-1677.

The Chicago-style hot dog ranks with deep-dish pizza as a source of local
culinary pride, and this busy stand serves up some of the best in town. Though
topping choices vary depending on individual taste, the Chicago-style dog
(known as a "red hot") typically consists of a Vienna beef frank served on a
poppy-seed bun. Mustard, relish and onions are a must, and tomatoes, pickle
slices, cucumber, lettuce and both green and hot peppers are often added, along
with a dash of celery salt. Ketchup, however, has no business on a red hot!

Green Door Tavern $ American

678 N. Orleans St., River North. 312-664-5496. www.greendoorchicago.com.

Constructed only one year after the
Chicago Fire of 1871, this is among the
oldest downtown buildings and shows its
age in a 10-degree list to the right and
sloping floors. It's been a tavern since 1921
and today serves good burgers, sandwiches (try the triple-decker grilled
cheese), and 35 different kinds of beer.

Half Shell $ Seafood

676 W. Diversey Pkwy., Lincoln Park. 773-549-1773.

This quintessential neighborhood dive is located below street level; its down-
scale atmosphere is at odds with its surroundings. Though small and dark, Half
Shell lures loyal locals craving fresh crab legs, shrimp, oysters and fried seafood for lunch or dinner. Diners are welcome to belly up to the curving bar,
which takes up half the room, rather than wait for a table.

Healthy Food $ Lithuanian

3236 S. Halsted St., Bridgeport. 312-326-2724.

Don't let the name fool you; they don't serve health food here. What they do
offer is yummy Lithuanian home cooking. Traditional folk art decorates the
walls and the menu offers a mix of specialties, vegetarian entrées and some
American favorites. Breakfast is best and the *blynais* (pancakes served with
sour cream), smeared with chunky fruit compote, are to die for.

Hema's Kitchen $ Indian

6406 N. Oakley Ave., West Rogers Park. 773-338-1627. www.hemaskitchen.com.

Hema Potla and her family prepare awesome home-cooked Indian food in her
little Far North Side restaurant. The wait can be awesome, too, especially on
weekends, so be prepared. You can BYOB to enjoy while you wait. So popular
has Hema's cooking become that she's opened another spot in Lincoln Park at
2411 N. Clark Street *(773-529-1705).*

Lou Mitchell's $ American

565 W. Jackson Blvd,. Near West Side. 312-939-3111.

The place for breakfast (you can get lunch,
too) in downtown Chicago since 1923, Lou
Mitchell's still serves up manly portions of
oatmeal, eggs, pancakes, French toast and
fluffy over-stuffed omelets to satisfy the
heartiest appetites. Don't mind the plastic
plants and the no-nonsense service.

Mr. Beef

$ Italian

666 N. Orleans St., River North. Lunch Mon–Sat. Closed Sun. 312-337-8500.

Tonight Show host Jay Leno put this place on the map. He discovered it as a struggling stand-up comic working the nightclub circuit and has been recommending it to his Hollywood pals for years. Go to Mr. Beef for the Italian beef sandwiches, consisting of a soft Italian roll piled high with thinly sliced marinated beef garnished with giardinere (pickled peppers, celery and spices).

The Third Coast

$ American

1260 N. Dearborn St., Gold Coast. 312-649-0730. www.3rdcoastcafe.com.

Sip cappuccino or claret in this warm, comfortable coffeehouse and wine bar, which is open early and into the wee hours. The clientele here ranges from well-dressed Gold Coast matrons to bohemian art students who stay at the Three Arts Club across the street. Good, light fare includes soups, sandwiches and salads. It's a nice place to meet for lunch.

Twin Anchors Restaurant-Tavern

$ Barbecue

1655 N. Sedgwick St., Old Town. 312-266-1616. www.twinanchorsribs.com.

Beloved for its succulent, melt-in-your-mouth ribs, Twin Anchors has been a popular pub since it opened after Prohibition; Frank Sinatra stopped here regularly in the 1960s. The essential neighborhood joint with its relaxed and modest atmosphere makes a nice escape from upscale chic.

Wishbone

$ Southern

1001 W. Washington Blvd., Near West Side. No dinner Mon. 312-850-2663. www.wishbonechicago.com.

Have a heaping helping of hoppin' John or mix and match down-home side dishes with blackened catfish and chicken étoufée. Wishbone's colorful, lively dining room attracts an eclectic crowd, from kids to celebrities, and serves a hearty Cajun breakfast as well. There's another location at 3310 N. Lincoln Avenue *(773-549-2663).*

Wow Bao

$ Asian

835 N. Michigan Ave., in Water Tower Place, Magnificent Mile. Open daily 10:30am–8:30pm. 312-642-5888. www.wowbao.com.

If you want a quick bite while you're shopping on Mag Mile, Wow Bao serves up fresh steamed buns (bao) to business-lunchers and shoppers alike from their take-out booth just inside the Chicago Water Tower. Asian buns are served hot and stuffed with such combinations as Kung Pao chicken, spicy Mongolian beef, and green vegetables. Wash your selection down with ginger ale made with fresh ginger, or hibiscus iced tea. Rice bowls, salads and soups are also available.

Dining in Oak Park and Evanston
Moderate

Café le Coq $$$ French
734 Lake St., Oak Park. 708-848-2233.

This tiny gem has become a destination for Chicago gourmets. The cozy place seats 75 and serves bistro favorites such as mussels in white wine, filet of sole stuffed with shrimp soufflé, and duck à l'orange for two. Service is efficient and friendly, and the atmosphere conjures up late-19C Paris. The list of French wines (more than 60 labels) includes some good lesser-known vintages.

Trio Atelier $$$ French
1625 Hinman Ave., Evanston. Dinner only. Closed Mon. 847-733-8746. www.trio-restaurant.com.

Located in the lobby of The Homestead hotel *(see Must Stay)*, **Trio Atelier** ranks among the area's finest restaurants. Diners can tailor their meal to their appetite here with Trio's selection of petite (intended to spark the palate), medium and large (entrée-size) "tastes."

Inexpensive

Avenue Ale House $$ American
825 S. Oak Park Ave., Oak Park. 708-848-2801. www.avenuealehouse.com.

A pub, yes, but you wouldn't know from the grub. The large, comfortable tavern features an array of steaks and chops, salmon and shrimp, burgers and sandwiches, served elegantly and in large portions. Live music entertains Thursday through Saturday nights, and you can catch a game on the TVs in the bar. In summer, rooftop dining makes the Avenue Ale House a neighborhood favorite.

Davis Street Fishmarket $$ Seafood
501 Davis St., Evanston. 847-869-3474. www.davisstreetfishmarket.com.

Forget those warnings you got about not ordering seafood in the Midwest. This unpretentious joint serves delicious, simply prepared fish and shellfish from the ocean, gulf and Great Lakes. Decorated in a funky Key-West-meets-Nantucket style, the fishmarket forsakes haute cuisine for broiled, baked, sautéed, steamed, blackened or fried fish, served with redskin potatoes and corn on the cob.

Tapas Barcelona $$ Spanish
1615 Chicago Ave., Evanston. 847-866-9900. www.tapasbarcelona.com.

Colorful and noisy, Tapas Barcelona serves excellent "little plates," paellas, sandwiches and even pizzas with an Iberian flare. Don't miss the *datiles con tocino*, a sinful concoction of baked fresh dates wrapped with bacon in a bell-pepper sauce. Reasonably priced Spanish wines are available by the glass or bottle, along with ports, sherries and other cordials.

Another Way to Look at It: Restaurants by Theme

Looking for the best restaurant for your special occasion? Want to see that star chef from the Food Network? In the preceding pages, we've organized the eateries by price category, so below we've broken them out by theme to help you plan your meals while you're in town. *Restaurants listed below are in Chicago unless otherwise noted.*

Breakfast Spots
Ann Sather *(p 109)*
Healthy Food *(p 110)*
Lou Mitchell's *(p 110)*
Wishbone *(p 111)*

Easy on the Budget
Chicago Pizza and Oven Grinder *(p 109)*
Ed Debevic's *(p 109)*
Gold Coast Dogs *(p 109)*
Green Door Tavern *(p 110)*
Half Shell *(p 110)*
Healthy Food *(p 110)*
Hema's Kitchen *(p 110)*
Lou Mitchell's *(p 110)*
Mr. Beef *(p 111)*
The Third Coast *(p 111)*
Twin Anchors Restaurant–Tavern *(p 111)*
Wishbone *(p 111)*
Wow Bao *(p 111)*

Ethnic Experiences
Healthy Food *(p 110)*
Hema's Kitchen *(p 110)*
Pasteur *(p 109)*
Tizi Melloul *(p 106)*

Hippest Décor
Blackbird *(p 104)*
Green Zebra *(p 105)*

Neighborhood Favorites
Avenue Ale House (Oak Park) *(p 112)*
Bistro 110 *(p 104)*
Café Le Coq (Oak Park) *(p 112)*
Chicago Pizza and Oven Grinder *(p 109)*
Club Lucky *(p 108)*
Davis Street Fishmarket (Evanston) *(p 112)*
Erwin *(p 108)*
Half Shell *(p 110)*
Heaven on Seven *(p 108)*
Twin Anchors Restaurant–Tavern *(p 111)*

Places to Eat with Kids
Andies *(p 107)*
Brasserie Jo *(p 105)*
Ed Debevic's *(p 109)*
Gino's East *(p 108)*
Gold Coast Dogs *(p 109)*

Pre-theater Dining
Rhapsody *(p 106)*
Russian Tea Time *(p 106)*

Restaurants with History
The Berghoff *(p 107)*
Green Door Tavern *(p 110)*
The Pump Room *(p 105)*

Special-Occasion Restaurants
Ambria *(p 102)*
Arun's *(p 102)*
Charlie Trotter's *(p 103)*
Everest *(p 103)*
Pluton *(p 103)*
Spiaggia *(p 104)*
Topolobampo *(p 107)*
Trio Atelier (Evanston) *(p 112)*
Tru *(p 104)*

Small Plates (Tapas)
Cafe Ba-Ba-Reeba! *(p 107)*
Tapas Barcelona (Evanston) *(p 112)*

Star Chefs
Charlie Trotter's (Charlie Trotter) *(p 103)*
Everest (Jean Joho) *(p 103)*
Topolobampo (Rick Bayless) *(p 107)*
Tru (Rick Tramonto and Gale Gand) *(p 104)*

Steakhouses
Avenue Ale House (Oak Park) *(p 112)*
Harry Caray's *(p 105)*
Saloon Steakhouse *(p 106)*

The properties listed below were selected for their ambience, location and/or value for money. Prices reflect the average cost for a standard double room for two people in high season. High season in Chicago is summer; rates are considerably less in low season. Price ranges quoted do not reflect the Chicago hotel tax of 15.4%. For a list of hotels organized by theme (Posh Places, Hotels for Business, etc.), see p 125.

$$$$$	Over $350	**$$**	$100–$175
$$$$	$250–$350	**$**	Under $100
$$$	$175–$250		

Luxury

Four Seasons Hotel $$$$$ 343 rooms

120 E. Delaware Pl., Magnificent Mile. 312-280-8800 or 800-819-5053. www.fourseasons.com/chicagofs.

Done in lush fabrics, dark woods and rich colors, guest rooms wrap visitors in luxury with marble baths and thick terry robes. On the 32nd to 46th floors of the hotel, deluxe rooms afford sweeping views of Lake Michigan or the city skyline. For business travelers, "Executive-Tech" rooms feature additional data ports and a four-in-one fax machine/copier/scanner/printer. Work out in the newly expanded fitness facility, complete with an indoor pool. Once you've tired out those muscles, a trip to the hotel's urban spa might be in order. **Seasons Restaurant ($$$$)** serves contemporary American fare in its opulent dining room; Chicagoans love it for Sunday brunch. Adjoining **Seasons Lounge** is a perfect place for afternoon tea.

The Peninsula Chicago $$$$$ 339 rooms

108 E. Superior St., Magnificent Mile. 312-337-2888 or 866-288-8889. www.chicago.peninsula.com.

A new addition to Chicago's star-studded hotel lineup, the Peninsula (yes, as in the incomparable Hong Kong Peninsula) is indeed a luxurious stay. Quietly elegant, trim and classic, the hotel is nonetheless futuristic in its many appointments, which include steamless TV screens in the bathrooms. Spacious rooms, among the largest in the city, provide a minimum of 531 square feet. The hotel's acclaimed health facilities boast a stunning pool and the 14,000-square-foot **Peninsula Spa**, which takes up the top two floors of the hotel. And **Avenues ($$$$)** restaurant consistently rates among the best in Chicago. Afternoon tea is served in the soaring lobby as live string music drifts down from a tiny balcony that overlooks the room.

Amalfi Hotel $$$$ 215 rooms

20 W. Kinzie St., River North. 312-395-9000 or 877-262-5341. www.amalfihotelchicago.com.

At the Amalfi, your well-appointed room is your sanctuary, complete with Egyptian cotton linens, a pillow-top mattress and multihead shower. The concierge is your "Experience Designer"; he or she is available to consult with you upon arrival regarding all the hip things you want to do while you're in the neighborhood, and can be summoned throughout your visit to assist with crises or answer questions. While the hotel lacks a dining room, complimentary continental breakfast is served on each floor, and food can be ordered in from **Harry Caray's** restaurant *(see Must Eat)* across the street. **Keefers ($$$)**, on the first floor, serves splendid steaks and chops.

The Drake Hotel $$$$ 537 rooms

140 E. Walton Pl., Magnificent Mile. 312-787-2200 or 800-445-7667. www.thedrakehotel.com.

Since 1920, the Italian Renaissance-style limestone building at the north end of the Magnificent Mile has been *the* address for visiting celebrities *(see Neighborhoods/ Magnificent Mile)*. Antique solid-brass candelabras and the original mahogany ceiling inset with hand-painted tiles set the tone in the lobby. Rooms, some overlooking Lake Michigan, combine floral fabrics with dark woods. The old-fashioned (it opened in 1933) but respected **Cape Cod Room ($$$$)** serves—what else?—seafood at lunch and dinner in a business-casual atmosphere. The Drake is now a Hilton property. High Tea in the lovely Palm Court is a must while you're in Chicago *(see p 30)*.

The Fairmont Chicago $$$$ 692 rooms

200 N. Columbus Dr., Loop. 312-565-8000 or 800-866-5577. www.fairmont.com/chicago.

Rising just east of Millennium Park, the Fairmont has long provided a home away from home for political figures and celebrities. Spacious rooms are well appointed with soothing colors and contemporary style; you'll have your choice of city or lake views. Guests have access to the luxurious Lakeshore Athletic Club next door, with its six floors of workout facilities, including a 110-foot-high climbing wall and an eight-lane pool. And for business travelers, there's a full-service business center on-site. Tea is served each afternoon in the Lobby Lounge. This is a great location for attending summer music festivals in the lakeside parks *(see Calendar of Events)*.

InterContinental Chicago $$$$ 807 rooms

505 N. Michigan Ave., Magnificent Mile. 312-944-4100 or 800 327-0200. www.chicago.intercontinental.com.

This Mag Mile classic began life as a men's club in 1929 and still retains many of the club's original decorative embellishments *(see Neighborhoods/Magnificent Mile)*. Egyptian, Renaissance and Middle Eastern motifs ornament public spaces and ballrooms, giving the public areas a thoroughly exotic ambience, and lavish majolica tile sets off the hotel's celebrated junior Olympic-size swimming pool. South tower rooms are furnished in elegant Biedermeier style and have the best views; those in the north tower sport a more modern look. Dine on regional American dishes at **Zest ($$$)**, which has been remodeled with minimalist panache.

W Chicago Lakeshore $$$$ 556 rooms

644 N. Lakeshore Dr., Gold Coast. 312-943-9200 or 888-625-5144. Also at 172 W. Adams St., Loop. www.starwoodhotels.com.

Overlooking the lakefront, W's "spectacular" rooms afford great views of Navy Pier and the lake beyond, while those dubbed "wonderful" face the cityscape. With serenity in mind, the décor takes something of a Zen twist in its deep colors and strong lines. Rooms come equipped with electronic amenities including CD/DVD players, with a 24-hour CD library at your service.

Wheeler Mansion $$$$ 11 rooms

2020 S. Calumet Ave., Near South Side. 312-945-2020. www.wheelermansion.com.

A stay here will give you a glimpse into life on Chicago's once-elegant Near South Side. Built in 1870, just a year before the Chicago Fire, this landmark is located in the Prairie Avenue Historic District, not far from Glessner House *(see Historic Sites)*. Individual room decorations suggest a 19C style, with dark wood trim, antique queen beds and marble baths, all private. The house is conveniently located for South Side activities, including conventions at McCormick Place, and is not far from the lakefront. Complimentary gourmet breakfast and parking are included with your reservation.

Moderate

Allerton Crowne Plaza $$$ 443 rooms

701 N. Michigan Ave., Magnificent Mile. 312-440-1500 or 800-227-6963. www.crowneplaza.com.

The Allerton has served Chicago as a hotel since 1924, and a renovation has nicely restored its original polish inside and out. Guest rooms are outfitted with marble baths and glow with warm wood tones and a rich palette of wall and fabric colors. Check out the view from the top-floor fitness center. The famous Tip-Top-Tap that once occupied the 23rd floor has been moved to the second floor and transformed into **Taps on Two ($$$)** French bistro.

Hard Rock Hotel $$$ 381 rooms

230 N. Michigan Ave., Loop. 312-345-1000. www.hardrockhotelchicago.com.

Smack dab between the Loop and the Mag Mile, this brand-new property has convenience and a lot more going for it. The jazzy Art Deco Carbide and Carbon building has been skillfully converted to accommodate this cool new hotel. Integrating the best of the old with a bit of new dazzle, including a moderate number of rock 'n' roll artifacts, the Hard Rock manages a high degree of sophistication. Modern guest-room amenities include flat-screen TVs, DVD/CD 5-disc changers, free high-speed Internet access and dual-line phones. It's a convenient walk from here to the many attractions up and down Michigan Avenue, as well as east to the lakefront and along the river.

Hotel 71 $$$ 454 rooms

71 E. Wacker Dr., Loop. 312-346-7100 or 800-621-4005. www.hotel71.com.

Billing itself as an "urban hotel adventure," 71 has given a tired 1950s hotel an extreme makeover. Though the facade retains a dated look, the interior public spaces and rooms have been boldly and freshly redone with upbeat colors, animal prints and ultra-suede, and sleek furniture. Light sculptures add a chic touch. Rooms on the north side overlook the Chicago River.

The House of Blues Hotel $$$ 367 rooms

333 N. Dearborn St., River North. 312-245-0333 or 877-569-3742. www.loewshotels.com.

Forget English-manor style and French-country charm, the House of Blues Hotel aims to rock your world. Flamboyantly decorated throughout, the hotel makes a fitting partner for the exuberant **House of Blues** restaurant/nightclub next door *(see Nightlife)*. Located along the Chicago River in landmark Marina City, the HOB complex also includes a 36-lane bowling alley, boat charters, a health club, a wine bar and an upscale steakhouse.

Hyatt Regency Chicago $$$ 2,019 rooms

151 E. Wacker Dr., Loop. 312-565-1234 or 800-633-7313. www.chicagoregency.hyatt.com.

If you're a Hyatt fan, welcome to the Mothership. This is the chain's largest property, and it's a behemoth. The glass-enclosed lobby, set about with greenery and fountains, can be something of an oasis, and the hotel's Big Bar sports the longest freestanding bar in North America, if such things matter. (As you might imagine, it serves everything BIG.) Its huge windows also offer good views looking north over the river. The hotel's location on East Wacker makes it convenient to destinations on both sides of the river, as well as Millennium Park and the lakefront. Chicago has several other Hyatt hotels as well.

Le Meridien
$$$ 311 rooms

521 N. Rush St., Magnificent Mile. 312-645-1500 or 800-543-4300. www.lemeridienhotels.com.

With Nordstrom—including Nordstrom Spa—and the entire North Bridge mall at your doorstep, the shopper staying at Le Meridien wants for nothing (you don't even need to go outside to reach the mall). Of course, the hotel is convenient to the entire Mag Mile, and its opulence is contemporary and understated with honey-tone woods, neutral colors and clean lines. Le Meridien's restaurant, **Cerise ($$$)**, is worth seeking out, as it's rarely crowded and serves good French fare. Find Cerise on the hotel's lobby floor, five stories up.

Palmer House Hilton
$$$ 1,639 rooms

17 E. Monroe St., Loop. 312-726-7500 or 800-445-8667. www.hiltonchicagosales.com.

Famous for its stunning hand-painted Beaux Arts ceiling, Empire Ballroom and lobby space, this Chicago fixture is dusting itself off with an interior renovation. The hotel's site on the corner of State Street in the Loop is convenient to shopping, dining, theater, Millennium Park and the Art Institute, making it a favorite among conventioneers and visitors interested in downtown attractions. The Palmer House features **Trader Vic's Restaurant ($$$)**, something of a historic attraction itself for its oh-so-1950s Polynesian umbrella drinks.

Silversmith Crowne Plaza
$$$ 143 Rooms

10 S. Wabash Ave., Loop. 312-372-7696 or 800-227-6963. www.crowneplaza.com.

Tucked into Jeweler's Row just feet from the elevated tracks, the beautifully appointed Silversmith comes as an elegant surprise. Built in 1897 as a warren for jewelry makers, the National Historic Landmark has been converted into a hotel and renovated in late 19C Arts and Crafts style. Rich oak paneling, glazed terra-cotta and Stickley furnishings throughout make a nice change from both hotel modern and B&B flounce. Don't be put off by the hotel's proximity to the elevated tracks; windows have been soundproofed. For extra quiet, however, ask for a room closer to the 10th floor.

Sofitel Chicago Water Tower
$$$ 415 rooms

20 E. Chestnut St., Magnificent Mile. 312-324-4000 or 800-763-4835. www.sofitel.com.

The talk of all the architectural circles, the dramatic upside-down exterior and slick, too-cool interior of the new Sofitel live up to the buzz. The techno-hip lobby employs decorative lighting and artwork to distinct advantage, and the rooms carry through with sophisticated contemporary European styling. Sofitel's sleek brasserie, **Café des Architectes ($$$)**, serves seafood and other dishes accented with Mediterranean, Asian and Latin American flavors.

Swissôtel $$$ 632 rooms

323 E. Wacker Dr., Loop. 312-565-0565 or 800-637-9477. www.chicago.swissotel.com.

Designed by prominent Chicago architect Harry
Weese, the Swissôtel cuts a crisp and shimmering
43-story silhouette, its crisp triangular shape
wrapped entirely in glass. The property exudes a
quiet elegance, and the best thing about its spacious, well-appointed rooms (besides the door-
bells) is the magnificent view from every one. The

Penthouse Health Club and Spa, one of the largest in a Chicago hotel, boasts
all the necessities: lap pool, sauna, steam room and whirlpool. Swissôtel caters
largely to corporate travelers, so its business amenities—meeting spaces, a
business center, secretarial services and so on—are second to none.

Talbott Hotel $$$ 147 rooms

20 E. Delaware Pl., Magnificent Mile. 312-944-4970 or 800-825-2688.
www.talbotthotel.com.

Snug and intimate with an English fox-hunting theme,
the tony Talbott features antiques and two fireplaces
in its wood-paneled Victorian lobby. Guest rooms and
suites, some with full kitchens, are simply but taste-
fully appointed in period reproductions. The hotel's
overall tranquility transports guests far from the
bustle of nearby Michigan Avenue, and the concierge
can help with anything from procuring theater tickets to setting up a meeting.
Guests here also enjoy nightly turndown service and complimentary access to the
72,000-square-foot Gold Coast Multiplex fitness facility.

The Whitehall Hotel $$$ 221 rooms

105 E. Delaware Pl., Magnificent Mile. 312-944-6300 or 800 948-4255.
www.hotelwhitehallchicago.com.

Just steps off the north end of Mag Mile (one block south of haute-couture shopping
on Oak Street; *see Must Shop*), this venerable inn is among the original small hotels
in the city, serving an elite clientele since 1974. Today it retains its polish thanks to a
renovation that has refreshed its English country-manor atmosphere. Light-filled
rooms are done in neutral tones offset by dark period furnishings. The attentive staff
provides personalized service, and small pets (under 30 pounds) are accepted.

Inexpensive

Best Western Hawthorne Terrace $$ 59 rooms

3434 N. Broadway, Lakeview. 773-244-3434 or 888-860-3400. www.hawthorneterrace.com.

Nestled in a neighborhood on Chicago's North Side, the Hawthorne Terrace
offers a charming boutique ambience convenient to Wrigley Field and the
lakefront. Rooms have a vintage feel, with flowered wallpaper and bedspreads;
many come equipped with whirlpool tubs, refrigerators and microwaves, and
garden views. Enjoy a complimentary continental breakfast with your newspaper each morning. There's even a small workout room.

Must Stay: Chicago Area Hotels

Chicago's Lenox Suites Hotel $$ 324 rooms

616 N. Rush St., Magnificent Mile. 312-337-1000 or 800-445-3669. www.lenoxsuites.com.

Location, location, location. A good property for families, Lenox studios and suites offer a little more space than a standard hotel room, plus refrigerators and microwaves, in a basic, down-to-earth setting just a block off the Mag Mile. A complimentary continental breakfast is even delivered to your room in the morning. The new 16th-floor Premier Level has been refurbished with bright fabrics and high-speed Internet connection in each suite.

City Suites Hotel $$ 45 Rooms

933 W. Belmont Ave., Lakeview. 773-404-3400 or 800-248-9108. www.cityinns.com.

City Suites inhabits a neighborhood that bustles with street life day and night, crowded as it is with restaurants, bars, nightclubs and even a tattoo parlor. Most of the units in this Art Deco restoration are suites furnished with hide-a-beds and refrigerators, though some standard queen rooms are available for less. Unexpected amenities such as refrigerators, shaving/make-up mirrors and robes make City Suites a good bet for the price. The elevated train just west provides rapid transportation to downtown.

The Essex Inn $$ 267 rooms

800 S. Michigan Ave., Grant Park. 312-939-2800 or 800-621-6909. www.essexinn.com.

Though its rooms are basic, the Essex appeals for its good prices and convenient location along South Michigan Avenue. A recent renovation added a garden pool and fitness center on the fourth-floor rooftop. Across the street, Grant Park makes a lovely front yard, and the hotel is within walking distance of the Loop, Millennium Park, the lakefront and Art Institute.

Fitzpatrick Chicago $$ 140 rooms

166 East Superior St., Magnificent Mile. 312-787-6000 or 800-367-7701.
www.fitzpatrickhotels.com.

With three properties in Ireland and three in the US, the Fitzpatrick Hotel Group cultivates a blend of traditional Euro and American styles, with a touch of the Celtic. In Chicago, the hotel's warm gold-tone lobby exudes the intimate feeling of a boutique hotel in size and décor. The Fitzpatrick features 100 suites with king or queen beds and queen sleeper beds in the sitting rooms. Kings or doubles furnish the 300-square-foot "executive rooms," and all accommodations include a wet bar along with two phone lines, wireless Internet access and data ports. Enjoy the all-day Irish breakfast in the restaurant, or go downstairs to **Fitzers** pub for a bit of Irish hospitality and a draft.

Hotel Allegro Chicago

$$ 483 rooms

171 W. Randolph St., Loop. 312-236-0123 or 866-672-6143. www.allegrochicago.com.

Bold colors and prints have transformed the North Loop theater district's 1926 Bismarck Hotel into a stylish Hollywood set. The lobby's fluted glass and oak-paneled walls are the backdrop for cobalt-blue velvet chaise loungues and red velour sofas. Guest rooms sport contemporary colors (pumpkin-colored walls and oversize upholstered brown and cream headboards) and modern amenities (a Sony sound system, a flat-screen

TV and wireless high-speed Internet access). Traveling with your pet? Dogs and cats are welcome at Hotel Allegro, which even offers special packages for pets and their humans.

Hotel Burnham

$$ 122 rooms

1 W. Washington St., Loop. 312-782-1111 or 877-294-9712. www.burnhamhotel.com.

Designed by Daniel Burnham's architectural firm in 1895, the historic **Reliance Building**★★ *(see p 25)* was restored in 1999 as the fanciful Hotel Burnham. Here original design elements, such as the mosaic floor and ornamental metal elevator grilles, blend with bold interior stylings, including royal-blue velvet headboards and matching cornices in the guest rooms. Conveniently located for shoppers, across from Marshall Field, the Burnham is also within walking distance of theaters, the Art Institute, Millennium Park and the lakefront. Enjoy American comfort food in the hotel's **Atwood Café ($$$)**.

Hotel Monaco

$$ 192 rooms

225 N. Wabash Ave., Loop. 312-960-8500 or 866-610-0081. www.monaco-chicago.com.

Two blocks from the Loop or the Mag Mile, this boutique property was designed as the world traveler's 1930s Art Deco-style living room. In the oversize lobby, the registration desk is modeled after a classic steamer trunk. Guest rooms are done in dark woods and pistachio green in the French Deco style. Whimsical amenities include an in-room pet goldfish on request and "tall" rooms with 9-foot beds and extra-high showerheads. If you're traveling with your entourage, check out the Rock Star Suite; it has hosted the likes of James Taylor and Britney Spears. In a bit of a contrast, down-home all-American cooking—including a red-wine-glazed meatloaf "TV dinner"—is available next door at **South Water Kitchen ($$)**.

Majestic Hotel

$$ 53 rooms

528 Brompton Ave., Lakeview. 773-404-3499 or 800-727-5108. www.cityinns.com.

Going to a Cubs game? Located steps from Wrigley Field, as well as Lincoln Park and Belmont Harbor, this comfortable English-style inn is nicely situated for North Side activities. Of the 53 units, 22 are suites that include refrigerators, microwaves and wet bars. Amenities include robes, morning newspaper and a continental breakfast served in the lobby each morning. Prices dip considerably in the low season.

Millennium Knickerbocker Hotel $$ 305 rooms

163 E. Walton Pl., Magnificent Mile. 312-751-8100 or 866-266-8086. www.millenniumhotels.com.

Transformed several times since its construction in 1927, the Knickerbocker has most recently undergone a $35 million renovation. Its distinctive cathedral-style windows and lit marquee welcome guests as they did in Prohibition-era Chicago, and the breathtaking, 5,000-square-foot Crystal Ballroom (now used for meetings and special events) still echoes with the sounds of the Jazz Age. Rooms are small but comfortable. The **Martini Bar** serves 44 varieties of its namesake against a musical backdrop of live jazz piano.

The Raphael $$ 172 rooms

201 E. Delaware Pl., Magnificent Mile. 312-943-5000 or 800-983-7870. www.raphaelchicago.com.

Rustic Old World charm emanates from the beamed ceilings and arched windows of this small hotel located east of Michigan Avenue. Less showy than other Michigan Avenue boutique properties, the Raphael nonetheless offers a quiet stay in the heart of the city. Rooms are simple but spacious, featuring one king or two double beds.

Seneca Hotel $$ 160 rooms

200 E. Chestnut St., Magnificent Mile. 312-787-8900 or 800-800-6261. www.senecahotel.com.

Set in the shadow of the John Hancock Center, the venerable Seneca is a sturdy old residence hotel that offers travelers 160 rooms and suites with complete kitchens (including dishwashers) and comfortable rooms (100 additional rooms are reserved for residential guests.) A stay here is a little like visiting grandmother, in all the good ways: nothing too fancy but homey, sensible and well situated. Just a block east of Michigan Avenue, the Seneca is within walking distance of the Museum of Contemporary Art and all the shops of Water Tower Place, the Mag Mile and Oak Street. While it offers no dining facilities of its own, a deli, wine bar and the **Saloon Steakhouse** *(see Must Eat)* are located in the building, along with a full-service salon and spa.

Sutton Place Hotel $$ 246 rooms

21 E. Bellevue Pl., Magnificent Mile. 312-266-2100 or 866-378-8866. www.suttonplace.com.

Stylish and elegant, the modern 23-story Sutton Place caters to both business and getaway travelers. Comfortable rooms are custom-furnished with contemporary flair and a hint of Art Deco design; suites offer large living areas and wet bars. The marble baths are particularly nice here, with separate soaking tubs and showers. A full-service business center on the fourth floor offers everything from video-conferencing to document processing, and the sleek **Whiskey Bar** lounge is a perfect place to entertain clients.

The Tremont Hotel

$$ 130 rooms

100 E. Chestnut St. Magnificent Mile. 312-751-1900 or 800-621-8133. www.tremontchicago.com.

Another lodging in the English style, the Tremont is named for a "luxury" hotel that opened in 1838. Its cozy lobby, complete with a fireplace, welcomes guests with manor-house ambience; likewise the bright rooms and suites. The Tremont House next door offers 12 furnished suites with kitchens for those traveling with families or desiring a longer stay. Named for the infamous former coach of "Da Bears," **Mike Ditka's ($$$)** restaurant is located in the hotel, with downstairs dining (think steaks and chops) and a cigar bar on the second level.

The Willows Hotel

$$ 55 rooms

555 W. Surf St., Lincoln Park. 773-528-8400 or 800-727-3108. www.cityinns.com.

The Willows occupies a vintage 1920s building just off busy Broadway. Renovated in 19C French country style, the lobby is pretty in tones of pink and peach. Though bathrooms are small, the rooms are restful, done in a soft pastel palette. Not far away are Diversey Harbor, the Notebaert Nature Museum and Lincoln Park Zoo, along with shopping and dining on Broadway and surrounding blocks. Ask about the seasonal package deals.

Wooded Isle Suites

$$ 13 rooms

5750 S. Stony Island Ave., South Side. 773-288-8972 or 800-290-6844. www.woodedisle.com.

If you're planning to spend much of your visit around Hyde Park, these converted apartments might be most convenient for you. Located in a typical Chicago courtyard building, the 13 suites include one-bedroom apartments that sleep four or studios that sleep two in a Murphy bed. Separate eat-in kitchens add extra convenience. Steps away you'll find the University of Chicago, the Museum of Science and Industry and the beach. McCormick Place, the Museum Campus and the Loop are just a short hop away by car or public transportation.

Red Roof Inn

$ 208 rooms

162 E. Ontario St., Magnificent Mile. 312-787-3580 or 800-733-7663. www.redroof.com.

Who'd have guessed it? A reasonably priced, perfectly suitable hotel just off the Mag Mile in one of Chicago's hottest neighborhoods? With **Coco Pazzo Café ($$)**, a great little Italian bistro next door (try the fried calamari), you've got it made. Even if the room does remind you of your last road trip, your checkbook will be ahead of the game.

Staying in Oak Park and Evanston

The Carleton of Oak Park Hotel and Motor Inn $$ 154 rooms

1110 Pleasant St., Oak Park. 708-848-5000 or 888-227-5386. www.carletonhotel.com.

Opened in 1928 as Oak Park's "high-class hotel," the Carleton offers pleasant accommodations convenient to downtown Oak Park and about 20 minutes from the Loop via the nearby elevated train. Motor-inn rooms are slightly less in cost. Most rooms have microwaves and refrigerators. **Philander's Restaurant ($$)**, where nightly jazz accompanies hearty steaks and seafood dishes, is located in the lobby.

The Homestead $$ 90 rooms

1625 Hinman Ave., Evanston. 847-475-3300. www.thehomestead.net.

This colonial-style manse was built in 1928 as a genteel hotel "in a wonderful location." It still caters to both overnighters and extended-stay guests with single rooms, studios, and one- and two-bedroom apartments. Reservations include a continental breakfast and garage parking, and the rooms are simple but comfortable. The lakefront, downtown Evanston and the Northwestern University campus are all within walking distance, as is a wide variety of good places to eat. Best of all, **Trio Atelier** *(see Must Eat)*, among the area's finest restaurants, is located just off the lobby.

Hotel Orrington $$ 269 rooms

1710 Orrington Ave., Evanston. 847-866-8700 or 888-677-4648. www.hotelorrington.com.

After a $32 million renovation, the 1923 Orrington is freshly reopened. Retaining its lovely 1920s feel, the updated hotel now sports a fresh interior design and added amenities. All of its rooms, suites, banquet facilities and common areas have been refurbished and provisioned to please both vacation and business travelers and to attract meetings and 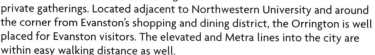 private gatherings. Located adjacent to Northwestern University and around the corner from Evanston's shopping and dining district, the Orrington is well placed for Evanston visitors. The elevated and Metra lines into the city are within easy walking distance as well.

The Write Inn $ 111 rooms

211 N. Oak Park Ave., Oak Park. 708-383-4800. www.writeinn.com.

This suburban inn is located along a shady stretch of residential street just steps from Oak Park's historic attractions and trains to the Loop. It sits across the street from the Hemingway Museum, and just north you'll find Hemingway's Birthplace. Decorated with 1920s period antiques, rooms range from small chambers outfitted with Murphy beds to larger rooms featuring sitting areas, whirlpool tubs and kitchenettes.

Another Way To Look At It: Hotels By Theme

Looking for good business hotels in Chicago? Want to bring Fido along? In the preceding pages, we've organized the properties by price category, so below we've broken them out by theme to help you plan your trip.

Hotels listed below are located in Chicago unless otherwise noted.

Closest Hotels to Wrigley Field
Best Western Hawthorne Terrace *(p 119)*
Majestic Hotel *(p 121)*

Easy on the Budget
The Carleton of Oak Park Hotel and
    Motor Inn (Oak Park) *(p 124)*
The Essex Inn *(p 120)*
Red Roof Inn *(p 123)*
The Write Inn (Oak Park) *(p 124)*

For Business Travelers
The Fairmont Chicago *(p 115)*
Four Seasons *(p 114)*
Hard Rock Hotel *(p 117)*
Hyatt Regency Chicago *(p 117)*
Le Meridien *(p 118)*
Millennium Knickerbocker Hotel *(p 122)*
Palmer House Hilton *(p 118)*
Sofitel Chicago Water Tower *(p 118)*
Swissôtel *(p 119)*
Sutton Place Hotel *(p 122)*

For Families
Chicago's Lenox Suites Hotel *(p 120)*
City Suites Hotel *(p 120)*
House of Blues Hotel *(p 117)*
Seneca Hotel *(p 122)*
The Tremont Hotel *(p 123)*
Wooded Isles Suites *(p 123)*

Hippest Décor
Hard Rock Hotel *(p 117)*
Hotel Allegro Chicago *(p 121)*
Hotel Monaco *(p 121)*
Hotel 71 *(p 117)*
House of Blues Hotel *(p 117)*
Sofitel Chicago Water Tower *(p 118)*

Hotels with History
The Drake Hotel *(p 115)*
The Homestead (Evanston) *(p 124)*
Hotel Burnham *(p 121)*
Hotel Orrington *(p 124)*
InterContinental Chicago *(p 116)*
Palmer House Hilton *(p 118)*

Silversmith Crowne Plaza *(p 118)*
Wheeler Mansion *(p 116)*
The Willows Hotel *(p 123)*

Near Mag Mile Shopping
Allerton Crowne Plaza *(p 116)*
Chicago's Lenox Suites Hotel *(p 120)*
The Drake Hotel *(p 115)*
Fitzpatrick Chicago *(p 120)*
Four Seasons Hotel *(p 114)*
InterContinental Chicago *(p 116)*
Le Meridien *(p 118)*
Millennium Knickerbocker Hotel *(p 122)*
The Peninsula Chicago *(p 114)*
The Raphael *(p 122)*
Red Roof Inn *(p 123)*
Seneca Hotel *(p 122)*
Sofitel Chicago Water Tower *(p 118)*
Sutton Place Hotel *(p 122)*
Talbott Hotel *(p 119)*
The Tremont Hotel *(p 123)*
The Whitehall Hotel *(p 119)*

Pet-Friendly Hotels
Hotel Allegro Chicago *(p 121)*
Hotel Monaco *(p 121)*
House of Blues Hotel *(p 117)*
Le Meridien *(p 118)*
Sofitel Chicago Water Tower *(p 118)*
W Chicago Lakeshore *(p 116)*
The Whitehall Hotel *(p 119)*

Posh Places
Amalfi Hotel *(p 115)*
The Drake Hotel *(p 115)*
The Fairmont Chicago *(p 115)*
Four Seasons Hotel *(p 114)*
InterContinental Chicago *(p 116)*
The Peninsula Chicago *(p 114)*

Spa Experiences
The Fairmont Chicago *(p 115)*
Four Seasons Hotel *(p 114)*
The Peninsula Chicago *(p 114)*
Swissôtel *(p 119)*

Index

The following abbreviations may appear in this Index: IN Indiana; NP National Park; SP State Park.

Index

Restaurants